Baby Miracles

INSPIRATIONAL TRUE TALES OF JOY AND NEW BEGINNINGS

Brad Steiger &
Sherry Hansen Steiger

▲

ADAMS MEDIA CORPORATION
Avon, Massachusetts

Dedication

We dedicate this book to our own beloved children—
Melissa, Julie, Kari, Steve, and Bryan, for making us proud
parents—and to their wonderful spouses, who are making
us proud grandparents.

Published by
Adams Media Corporation
57 Littlefield Street, Avon, MA 02322. U.S.A.
www.adamsmedia.com

ISBN: 1-58062-775-7

Printed in Canada.

J I H G F E D C B A

Library of Congress Cataloging-in-Publication Data
Steiger, Brad.
Baby miracles / Brad Steiger and Sherry Hansen Steiger.
        p.   cm.
ISBN 1-58062-775-7
1. Infants. I. Steiger, Sherry Hansen. II. Title.
HQ774.S815 2003
305.232—dc21
2003002611

This publication is designed to provide accurate and authoritative information with regard to
the subject matter covered. It is sold with the understanding that the publisher is not engaged
in rendering legal, accounting, or other professional advice. If legal advice or other expert
assistance is required, the services of a competent professional person should be sought.
        —From a *Declaration of Principles* jointly adopted by a Committee of the American Bar
        Association and a Committee of Publishers and Associations

While all the stories in this book are true, some of the names, dates, and places have
been changed to protect anonymity.

Illustration by ©Christie's Images / Superstock.

*This book is available at quantity discounts for bulk purchases.
For information, call 1-800-872-5627.*

Foreword

"Grown people may learn from little children, for the hearts of little children are pure, and therefore the Great Spirit may show to them many things which older people miss."
—Black Elk, Native American spiritual leader

We've all noticed this fascinating phenomenon. Hold up a baby or a photograph of a baby before an audience—almost any audience—and as if in a single voice everyone goes, "Ahhhhhhh."

This reverence for babies is hardwired into our brains. It is as if each new child born offers a promise and a hope that our species will survive on the planet and that we won't become extinct in spite of all the blunders that we adults make.

We're not surprised when even strangers on the

subway, bus, train, or plane grin widely and show us pictures of their new baby. And we know that their pride comes from far more than the knowledge that they have fulfilled their biological obligation. They have participated in the creation of a living, breathing miracle.

And who could argue that babies are not themselves tiny miracles? Each one is completely unique unto itself. There is no other human being exactly like this new little life. Look into their big open eyes and see a reflection of innocence, love, and peace—a living link between us and the angels.

And behold the miracles that babies work on their parents. Mothers learn patience, self-control, endurance, and most importantly, unconditional love. And mothers' arms become so strong that they can hold their precious burden longer than any father can. And all those guys who were searching for the true meaning of life suddenly understand what it's all about when they become fathers. They gain a fresh motive to work at their jobs and new social aims and moral impulses are born along with their baby.

Some women long to be mothers, dreaming about motherhood since they were children. One such little girl was Janice Gray Kolb, who was blessed with six children and experienced a miracle that saved her son's life.

Other couples, such as Matt and Susan, try and try

unsuccessfully for years to have children—and then one day Matt was given a sign in the very church where he and Susan were married that their prayers had been answered.

But in the midst of such joy and personal transformation life can sometimes deal what appears to be a very cruel blow of fate for the new baby and the proud parents. Terrible diseases and unexpected accidents that weren't in any parent's script for perfect happiness can suddenly intrude brutally upon a schedule that had seemed to be running along so well.

What can they do to preserve the tiny wellspring of joy that so illuminates their lives and is now so threatened by the shadow of death?

In the inspirational stories in this book, we present dramatic accounts of true miracles of faith, prayer, and courage that saved an injured, ill, or dying baby's life. In some instances, the skill of a brilliant doctor or surgeon challenged the odds to save the baby. In other remarkable cases, it would appear that a source of strength beyond that of human intervention occurred to prevent a tiny spark of love and light from being extinguished.

As parents ourselves, we have sat at the bedsides of our sick and injured children and asked for God's healing mercies to bless them and restore them to health.

As with mothers and fathers around the world, we know that our children are our legacy to the future, our guarantee that a physical aspect of ourselves will live on long after we have gone. As George Santayana observed, "Parents lend their children their experience and a vicarious memory; children endow their parents with a vicarious immortality."

SHERRY HANSEN STEIGER
BRAD STEIGER
Forest City, Iowa

Acknowledgments

We wish to thank the following individuals for their
assistance in gathering the inspirational stories for this
book: Matt Gildea, Jenny Stelnacker, Janice Gray Kolb,
Barbara May, Shirley Hessel, Linda Revere, and Dr.
P.M.H. Atwater. Those who wish to remain anonymous
or appear under pseudonyms know who they are and
receive equal thanks for their contributions.

*I*n 1996, Carol and Sam Odom, who now live in a suburb of Portland, Oregon, were very young newlyweds who discovered three months after their wedding day that Carol was pregnant.

Carol was nineteen and Sam was twenty. They had both wanted to continue taking college courses, and they had definitely not planned to begin a family until after they were much better established.

"It had seemed so romantic to be married while we were still in college," Carol said. "Sam had just completed his junior year and I was going to be a sophomore. We got married in August, shortly before the school year began. We were so happy and in love. And we resolved that now that we were married, we would really be able to concentrate on our studies, rather than daydreaming about when we would be able to spend time together on weekends."

But when she learned that she was pregnant, Carol knew that the timetable she and Sam had so carefully outlined for their future would be revised in short order. They would be forced to set romance aside and face the reality of being responsible grownups about to become parents.

"We are both very religious people," Carol explained. "Since we had been practicing birth control and I had nevertheless become pregnant, we believed that it was God's will that we should have a baby so soon in our marriage."

Carol and Sam decided that they would continue taking classes until the first semester ended in late December, and then they would both drop out of school. To help with the increased expenses of her maternity care, Carol would try to get a second part-time job in addition to the one she held as a clerk in a department store. Sam already had a nearly full-time job in a super-market, and he was certain that a garage owner who had served with his father in the military would give him a part-time job.

Carol and Sam read books on pregnancy and child-birth, and one evening a week they attended a Lamaze class. Lamaze allows both the expectant father and mother to learn about and understand the physical, mental, and emotional changes the female's body goes through, as well as trace the developmental stages of the fetus in order to better prepare for a healthy baby and delivery.

Having a baby is said to be the most difficult feat a human body will ever perform, yet we are not born with a "how to" manual. Giving birth to a baby is said to be harder than any Olympic challenge. Athletes prepare their bodies and work daily at strengthening and per-fecting their goals, yet women throughout history have performed the task of birthing a baby with little or no preparation.

"Several friends told us how much a prenatal course helped them, and they highly recommended it to us," Carol said. "It was a fabulous way for Sam and me to bond even further, and it made him feel more a part of the process that usually is focused on just the woman."

"Sam and I learned various relaxation and breathing exercises as well as muscle-strengthening exercises tar-geting the particular muscles and ligaments involved in supporting the growing baby and those that would be most active in the birthing process," Carol added.

Although she had experienced some morning sickness during the very early stages of her pregnancy, all in all, Carol expressed few complaints during the nine months of carrying their child. She had to drop her part-time job in a fast-food restaurant in her sixth month, but she continued in her position of clerk in the department store until two weeks before she delivered.

"We wanted to be surprised with the sex of our little miracle baby, so I didn't peek ahead of time with a sonogram or any other technical means of learning the gender of our unborn child," Carol said. "So when our son Wesley Samuel Odom was born, Aunt Gwen and my second cousin Elray won the family pool. Most of our relatives had bet on our having a girl, claiming something about my stubborn nature somehow being able to influence genetics."

The Odom's family physician, Dr. Colin Stevens, deemed the delivery quite effortless, especially for a first-time mother, and little Wesley appeared to be a strong, healthy child who had been born to loving parents. All went well with the baby until he was seven months old.

"Wesley hadn't even cried much during the night," Carol said. "We had really been spoiled by everything in our lives seeming to be so perfect. We were even in the process of making arrangements for my mother to sit with Wesley in the afternoons so I might get a part-time job to help with expenses."

The night before Carol's mother, Micki Boettcher, was to begin baby-sitting for the Odoms, Carol's stepfather, Dave Boettcher, was involved in a serious automobile accident. It appeared that he had fallen asleep while driving and had crossed the median line to run head-on into an approaching van. Dave was badly injured and charged with the responsibility for the accident, which had put the driver of the van and his wife in critical condition. Two of their three children had also been injured quite severely.

"Of course we knew that Mom could no longer sit for us," Carol said, "but we were more concerned that their insurance would not cover the expenses incurred by the accident. It also seemed very likely that the driver of the van would sue my stepfather, who was already charged with failure to control his vehicle and responsible for causing the accident."

Three days after Carol's stepfather entered the hospital, little Wesley began running a high fever.

"Both Sam and I tried to remain calm, trying to convince ourselves that it was no more than just the sniffles,"

Carol said. "I think we both feared that Wesley was really ill. Even after a couple of days when Wesley's breathing became more labored, we kept telling ourselves that it was only a mild congestion in the lungs that would soon pass. The truth was, neither one of us had any insurance. I was just about to start back to at least a part-time job with Mom's help baby-sitting Wesley before the accident, so I was still not working. We were so broke and in debt that we didn't have enough money to take him to the doctor. With only Sam's two part-time jobs, we had barely enough to pay the rent and squeeze by each month."

Sam's biological father had been placed in a veteran's hospital two years before the couple had married, and Sam's mother subsisted on a small military pension. Carol knew that her parents had no extra cash, and now that her stepfather lay in a hospital with a major lawsuit looming over him, they would be unable to lend them any money.

Sam and Carol put their arms around each other's shoulders and looked down on their son, red with fever and gasping for breath. Carol felt hot tears streaming down her cheeks.

"I don't know what to do," she said, unable to hold back her fear. "How can we help him?"

Sam suggested that they pray, and the two of them

got down on their knees next to Wesley's crib, beseech-
ing God to heal their son.

As fervent as their prayer may have been, Wesley's
labored gasping for breath did not lessen.

Carol sat all night at cribside, gently placing damp
washcloths on their son, hoping to lower the fever.

"Won't that make his sickness worse?" Sam said
when he got out of bed to join his wife at her vigil.
"Won't getting him wet like that only make him worse?"

Carol explained that she was doing her best to lower
the fever and that she believed that she was doing the
right thing. She told Sam to try to get to sleep, because
he had to be at work in two hours.

Later, as Sam was getting dressed and getting ready
to leave for his job at the supermarket, Carol cried out
that Wesley was turning blue and that he had stopped
breathing.

Sam stumbled against a chair, then sat down and
began to weep, asking God over and over to spare
their son.

With Wesley in her arms, Carol walked to the
kitchen and picked up the telephone, offering a silent
prayer that the telephone company had not yet made
good their threat to disconnect their line because of
delinquent bill payments. When she heard the dial tone,
she gave thanks to her guardian angel and dialed

Dr. Stevens's home number.

She offered another prayer when she realized that it was only 6:30 A.M. Hopefully, Dr. Stevens would be up having his first cup of coffee and not still be in bed. Carol knew from past experiences that Doc Stevens, now nearly seventy, could, on occasion, be rather cranky.

She breathed an audible sigh of relief when Dr. Stevens answered the phone in a tone that sounded as though he had already fortified himself with both coffee and breakfast.

"Dr. Stevens barely let me finish describing Wesley's illness when he began yelling at me for not having called him earlier," Carol said.

"When I explained our desperate financial situation, he snorted and told me not to worry about money over our baby's health. He said that if his word wouldn't establish our credit at the hospital, that he would just put it on his bill and we could pay him when we could afford it."

Following Dr. Stevens's instructions, Sam and Carol bundled Wesley up in a blanket and headed for the hospital in their car. As he had promised, a stern-faced Dr. Stevens was waiting for them in the emergency room, and he seemed almost to snatch Wesley out of Carol's arms and hand him over to a nurse.

"We dreaded registration at the desk," Carol said,

"because we had no insurance, as well as no money. We expected to be turned away and sent home with our baby, but the secretary just smiled and asked us to fill out a couple of forms giving consent for Wesley's treatment. We figured that Dr. Stevens had already cleared Wesley's admittance."

A few hours later, Carol and Sam stood as close as they were allowed to be, peering helplessly, but prayerfully, through the glass window where their tiny infant son lay still and unmoving—enclosed in an oxygen tent.

Dr. Stevens was grim-faced when he told them that Wesley may have been brought to the hospital too late for doctors or medicine to help him.

"We did all that we can do," Dr. Stevens said, placing a gentle hand on Carol's shoulder. "His lungs were terribly congested, and the fever had really taken its toll on his little body. It is now up to a higher power. Wesley is now completely in the hands of the angels."

Sam bowed his head and began to cry. Dr. Stevens squeezed Sam's shoulder with his other hand; then he said that he would leave the two of them alone with their son.

Almost in unison, Carol and Sam looked at one another and managed a tearful, but brave, smile. "It was as if we received the same message at precisely the same instant," Carol said. "It was as if an angel whispered in our ears and told us to pray as we had never prayed before for God to heal our son. We had said from the moment that I learned that I was pregnant that we knew that God wanted us to have this child. We knew then that He would not let Wesley die."

Sam and Carol clasped their hands in prayer and beseeched their God as never before. With all their hearts and souls, they asked God for a miracle healing for their little Wesley. They asked that he be allowed to live and to grow into a God-fearing man who would always walk a path of righteousness.

"After two or three minutes, I heard all around us, and reverberating throughout the hospital room, the most beautiful sound of a choir of lovely voices," Carol said. "Sometimes it seemed as if I could distinguish words—words such as 'glory,' and 'alleluia,' and 'holy, holy, holy.'

"I knew that Sam was also hearing the voices, because tears were streaming down his cheeks. I could tell by the expression on his face that these tears were different. We were hearing heavenly beings—angels, ministering to Wesley, healing him, with their beautiful voices."

When Dr. Stevens returned about fifteen minutes later, he checked Wesley's vital signs and smiled. "Remarkable," he said softly. "It seems impossible, but I see an improvement within the past half hour."

Two hours later, Dr. Stevens was ready to pronounce Wesley's signs of rapidly increasing recovery a genuine miracle.

"Strange and wonderful things like this sometimes happen," he said. "That's what keeps me going when I should be retired. I just have to stick around to see another healing miracle."

Carol acknowledges their debt to Dr. Stevens and modern medical treatment, but she said that she and Sam know that one of the greatest miracles came with the healing sounds provided by the angelic choir.

"God heard our prayers," she said, "and he sent his angels to heal Wesley."

Only two days later, Sam and Carol were able to take Wesley home. His lungs were completely clear and there were no adverse effects from the high fever that had seared his little body.

"As we were leaving the hospital, a small boy of eight or so approached us in a wheelchair," Carol said. "He told us that he was in the room close to Wesley's. He looked up at us wistfully and said that even though we were leaving, he hoped that he would still be able to hear the pretty music that came from the area where our baby was because when he listened to the music it made him feel good. It seems that he, too, had heard the angel choir and the sound of their healing voices."

On November 15, 2002, thirty-six-year-old twins Amanda and Meagen Baldwin each gave birth to a son. While this in itself is unique, it becomes even more bizarre when one considers that Amanda lives in Sydney, Australia, and Meagen resides in Belgium—approximately 12,000 miles apart. And when one learns that Amanda's son Truman was scheduled to be born on November 4, while Meagen's son Benjamin was penciled in on the calendar to be born in early December, the births of the two cousins on the very same day becomes downright eerie.

It all began when the twin sisters learned in late February that they were pregnant. Via e-mails and telephone calls, they joked about how bizarre it would be if they happened to give birth on the same day.

Amanda had to be induced when she was about eleven days overdue; and after a thirteen-hour labor, she gave birth to Truman at 1:06 A.M. on Friday, November 15. Shortly after it was certain that she had given birth without any further complications, her husband sent Meagen an e-mail.

And that's when things really got strange. As soon as Meagen in Belgium learned that Amanda in Australia had given birth, she began to feel nauseated. When she went to her doctor for a prenatal examination later that morning, Meagen was told that her baby could come at any time. That afternoon her water broke, and she went to the hospital where, at 2:40 A.M. on Friday, she gave birth to Benjamin, nearly a month before his due date.

When Meagen's husband called to tell Amanda and her family the news of Benjamin's birth, he could not resist saying that the two baby boys, though cousins in actuality, were really very much like twins. For, remarkably, those two first cousins, born 12,000 miles apart, will forever celebrate their birthdays on the same day, just as their mothers had always done.

*I*n June 1999, Anita
Stratton was walking
through a supermarket
parking lot, pushing a shopping cart with her right hand
and carrying ten-month-old Joan cradled in her left arm.
Two-year-old Larry followed close behind them, content-
edly sucking on the cherry lollipop that one of the store
managers had given him.

"It was a very warm day in the suburb of Memphis
where we lived," Anita says, "and after an hour of shopping for groceries in the crowded supermarket, I felt in
desperate need of a shower. Both of the kids were

fussing because it was their nap time, and I was really looking forward to putting them down, getting cleaned up, and relaxing for a half-hour or so before my husband, Wade, came home for dinner."

Although Anita doesn't bear any lasting ill will toward the driver of the van that struck them, she does feel that the woman was being very careless. "Because the lot was so crowded that afternoon, all drivers should have been extra cautious," Anita says. "We had just stepped off the sidewalk and had only taken a few steps into the parking lot when this woman in a large van seemingly came out of nowhere, driving really fast, heading right for us."

Anita managed to push Larry out of harm's way back onto the sidewalk, but the vehicle crashed into the shopping cart, tossing it aside, and slamming into Anita and her baby. In horror, she felt the impact tear Joan from her arms.

Anita was thrown to the rough cement of the parking lot, and she lay crumpled on her side, watching helplessly as baby Joan rolled under the van.

"What happened next will probably never leave my memory," Anita says. "I still view the scene over and over again in my nightmares. I saw one of the van's tires go right over Joan's head."

Anita screamed out in terror and anguish.

The driver of the van, realizing that she had struck a mother with her children, panicked and drove her vehicle into a wall of the supermarket.

Anita tried to get to her feet, then felt agonizing streaks of pain shoot up her leg. "I looked down and saw that shards of bone were sticking out from my right leg," she says, "but I had to get to my baby."

As brightly colored splotches of pain clouded her vision, Anita was dimly aware of one of the stock boys from the supermarket and a man kneeling beside her, telling her to lie still, that she might have internal injuries. Anita ignored them and began to crawl toward her baby.

"Another man and a woman stood over Joan, and I heard the woman scream in horror," Anita says. "I figured then that my baby was dead."

All around her men and women were shouting, milling about in confusion. "I knew the man trying to make me lie still was only doing what he thought was best," Anita said, "but I shook free of his hands and finally got to my little Joan."

Anita's voice still shakes as she recalls her first glimpse of her baby. "The whole side of her head was caved in," she said, "and she was just lying there with soft, whispery sighs and moans coming from her little mouth, her blue eyes rolling around looking for Mama."

The rest of that afternoon is pretty much a blur for Anita. She remembers crying over her terribly injured daughter, but retaining enough awareness not to try to pick her up.

"I remember the ambulance coming, and the paramedics working on Joan for a few minutes before they placed the three of us in the ambulance," Anita said. "I don't remember too much else until I woke up in a hospital bed with my leg in a cast and Wade beside me holding my hand."

As she regained consciousness, waves of grief overwhelmed her. "Our baby doll, Wade," she managed between sobs of dread and pain. "What about our beautiful Joanie?"

Wade had been crying, but he smiled broadly and pronounced the sweetest words that he could ever have spoken at that moment: "Honey, it's a miracle! Our baby is going to live!"

Incredibly, little Joan Stratton had suffered a crushed skull, a fractured pelvis, a punctured lung, and other broken bones, but she would live. According to the doctors at Children's Hospital, the elasticity of a ten-month-old child's skeletal structure and immediate medical treatment saved Joan's life. Although she suffered some nerve damage below the knee of her right leg and would quite likely have some facial scarring as a result of the damage to her skull, Joan's survival after such a serious accident was surely a miracle.

As a result of his mother's quick action in pushing him out of the way of the oncoming van, two-year-old Larry sustained only a number of bruises from sprawling on the sidewalk and hitting his head against a metal pole. The driver of the vehicle that had struck the Stratton family, a sixty-year-old woman, was charged with failure to have her vehicle under control, negligence, and causing severe injury to pedestrians. Fortunately for the Strattons, the woman's insurance covered most of their hospital bills.

*M*arie Jerrell, who lives in northern Missouri, told us that she had had her black Labrador, Buck, for fifteen years at the time when he performed the baby miracle that her family will never forget.

"I got Buck from my dad, Phil Ryan, on my sixteenth birthday," she said, "and the big old dog never left my side."

Marie's husband, Jake, also loved the dog, but when Buck began to develop the hip dysplasia problems that so frequently afflict larger dogs as they grow older, he suggested that she should put her beloved friend to sleep.

"Jake argued that Buck was obviously in a great deal of pain," Marie said, "and he reminded me how difficult it was for the old boy to get up and down. A couple of times when I had been walking Buck through the woods near our place, his back legs just seemed to go out on him and he fell down. I knew that Buck was probably suffering, but, selfishly or not, I couldn't bring myself to put him down."

Before Jake, Jr., was born in April of 2000, Marie's parents and brother Henry, as well as Jake, Sr., were concerned that Buck might be jealous of Marie's attentions and harm the baby when it came.

"My dad reminded me of his sister Sue who had to get rid of her German shepherd when my cousin Billy was born," Marie said. "And he pointed out that Aunt Sue had had Hans, her big shepherd, for only a couple of years—not fifteen, like I had had Buck—but Hans was so jealous of baby Billy that he knocked him out of his crib. Uncle Russ had sworn that Hans would have killed Billy if he hadn't been in the room and been able to restrain the animal. I remembered that Hans got put down the very next morning—without a trial or another chance."

Marie was very familiar with the account of Hans's

jealousy of Aunt Sue's baby, because her cousin Billy was now in his late twenties. The story had been told—as a cautionary tale regarding the danger of a dog becoming too possessive of its owner—many, many times in the Ryan family.

Marie assured everyone that she would be very alert toward even any minor changes in Buck's behavior. She knew that the dog would accept her baby and watch over him or her just as he had always been protective of her welfare.

On the second day after Little Jake was born and Marie and her son were released from the hospital, she presented Buck with the little bundle of humankind that would now demand her full attention.

"See, Buck," Marie spoke softly as the black Lab sniffed the baby and the blankets that swathed him. "This is Jake, my son. I know you will love and care for him as much as you have always loved and cared for me."

Buck whined, looked up at Marie with his kind, brown eyes, and seemed to understand completely exactly who the little newcomer was and what he meant to his beloved mistress.

When the baby was a couple of weeks old, the trucking firm that employed Jake as a long-distance hauler was forced to close down for a while. Although

they assured their drivers that the shutdown was temporary because of rising gas prices and a number of unexpected factors, Jake felt a great deal of stress and
anxiety.

"We don't have that much money in our savings
account," he told Marie one night as they were sitting
around the kitchen table deciding which bills needed to
be paid the soonest. "And look at these bills from the vet.
It seems like Buck needs five or six different prescrip-
tions refilled every month. He takes pills for his hips, for
his heart, for his lungs. . . . And now it's time for his
rabies shot again."

Marie knew what was coming, and she held Little
Jake closer to her, as if the mother-son bond would
ease the hurt of the words Big Jake was about to
speak: "Honey, we just can't afford to keep the old dog
any longer."

And she also knew what Jake would say next, pre-
senting her with the inevitable moment of decision, the
challenge of choice, Marie's choice: "We can't afford to
keep the dog and have enough money for Little Jake's
food and any medicine that he might need. You'll have to
choose Buck or Little Jake."

Marie went to bed, trying desperately to hold back
her tears. It made her cry even more when Buck whined
and worked his muzzle next to her face on the pillow,

checking to see if she was all right. It always upset the black Lab when she cried, and he had painfully pulled himself up from his big doggy basket at her side of the bed to try to comfort her.

That's when Marie made her choice: She would keep Buck and find a way to pay for his medicine without depriving Little Jake of anything that he might need.

The next day, Marie drove to a larger city near their small town and found a pawn shop. She managed to get some money toward the veterinarian's bill by pawning her class ring, her saxophone, and some jewelry that her grandmother had left her.

Big Jake had acted displeased when he found out what she had done, but he hugged Marie and told her sadly that the small sum that she had received for pawning her valuables wouldn't contribute a great deal toward Buck's continuing maintenance. She would have to make up her mind to put him to sleep.

The next week, Jake began a temporary job in the city, working as a stock man in a shipping company. It was the night shift, which meant that he would be gone five nights a week until eight o'clock in the morning, but it was the best that he could do. Marie asked him to reconsider, reminding him of the trucking firm's promise to put their drivers back to work in a few months, but Jake told her firmly that their meager savings could not last for very much longer. Plus, he argued, what if the trucking firm was unable to make good their word to put him back on the long-distance route? He couldn't afford to wait for someone to honor their well-intentioned promise and start looking for work when the Jerrell family was completely broke.

Marie was pleased that her husband was so conscientious, but now that he would be gone nights, she was really grateful for old Buck watching out for her and Little Jake.

When Little Jake was a month old, Marie was awakened around three in the morning by Buck punching her with his muzzle and making strange moaning sounds.

Marie sat up, wondering what was happening. Did Buck have to go outside?

Buck opened his mouth wide and gently closed it around Marie's wrist. "Firmly, but without hurting me, Buck tugged me to my feet," she said. "He kept making that funny moaning sound, and he led me to Little Jake's crib. At first my baby looked all right in the glow from the nightlight, but then I felt him and he seemed not to be breathing."

Marie turned on the overhead light and felt her heart pound in her chest. Little Jake had turned blue and stopped breathing.

"I had read and heard about Sudden Infant Death

Syndrome," Marie said, "and I was so frightened that I could barely make the 911 call for help."

Although it seemed to take hours for the paramedics to arrive with an ambulance, Marie was pleased to tell us that this story had a happy ending.

"Because Buck had sensed that something with Little Jake was just not right and had awakened me and pulled me to the crib, the paramedics got our son to the hospital in time and revived him before any permanent brain damage had been done," Marie said.

"Thank God, Little Jake never had another episode like that and Buck was now the hero in everyone's eyes that he had always been in mine. Buck lived another seven months before he went home to Doggy Heaven."

att said that he and his wife, Susan, will never forget December 27, 1998. "Susan and I had just completed another hectic Christmas season," he said. "We are both from very large families. Susan is one of eight, and I am one of nine. For us, the holiday season means lots of running from house to house, ensuring that we see every family member during this wondrous time of year. So two days after Christmas, I was preparing for a sales meeting in the usual way— shower, shave, and a brief rehearsal of my presentation. The next moment changed our lives forever."

We'll let Matt tell the story in his own words:

Susan and I were married on May 21, 1994. Both of us had been born and raised on the South Shore of Massachusetts, but due to my career, we would first reside in New Hampshire. The first measure of business in our "grand plan" was to start a family as soon as possible. But then there were promotions and relocations. Soon our address read Oak Creek, Wisconsin, and my career was in full bloom at Western Publishing.

On May 21, 1995, we made the ultimate decision to start a family. Given the fact that we were bred from such fertile family backgrounds, Susan and I thought that having a baby would be the easiest of all of our goals to accomplish. Nothing was further from the truth. Our journey to parenthood was just beginning.

Month after month of "practicing" to make a child, we both became frustrated and depressed. With each negative pregnancy test, our frustrations increased.

I remember the next scene as if it happened yesterday. I was changing clothes in our bedroom when Susan uttered the words that captured our frustrations: "Matt, I have to be pregnant."

I asked, "Why do you *have* to be pregnant?"

Susan, searching for the right words, finally answered, "Because it will complete me as a woman."

Susan and I had made a commitment before God to

stick by each other through sickness and health, good times and bad. We could not let Him down now — although we knew full well that we needed His guidance to see us through the woods.

Two years of frustration, tears, and desperation led us to Massachusetts General Hospital in Boston. We began meeting with a fertility doctor and his staff. Susan and I agreed this was the next necessary step to take.

But test after humbling test revealed that there nothing was wrong with any of either of our reproductive functions. We were just missing the "target."

Could it be that our faith in the Lord was being tested? Was it His plan that we would remain childless? Or was it that we were to adopt? We kept asking Him to show us what His plan was for us.

The first step in our fertility test was that Susan was put on the drug Clomid in order to intensify her ovulation period. This drug proved unsuccessful for us.

Next was an injection I had to administer to Susan. And this is where doubt started to cloud our vision of pregnancy.

It was May 1998 when the injections began — Step Two of a three-step program. The injected drug's purpose was to increase the likelihood of conception. However, the only thing it increased was our hatred of health insurance since it had a price tag of over $2,200 per month and was not covered by our insurance.

It was right then that we turned the process completely over to the Lord. If parenthood was in God's plans for us, we both prayed that we would conceive a child soon.

In mid-November of 1998 when I was attending the five o'clock sacrament at our parish, something amazing happened during the offertory period of the sacrament, the time when the Host is brought to the altar and the collection takes place. Typically, a hymn is sung during this portion of the mass, and on this day the selection happened to be a hymn that was very special to me. It was the same hymn that I heard at church that day when I was contemplating asking for Susan's hand in marriage. Something powerful was happening. I just knew some "thing" would be happening to us soon.

December 27, 1998, changed our lives forever. I was preparing for a sales meeting. While I was shaving, Susan called downstairs to tell me that I had forgotten to open my last Christmas present.

In disbelief, I questioned what she was saying. Then she entered our bathroom with the most wonderful present—a positive pregnancy test. Our prayers had been answered. Matthew Gerard, Jr., was born on August 23, 1999. Four long years of trials, tribulations, and frustrations were finally over.

Our family has extended since then. Our next pregnancy resulted in miscarriage and a pain that cannot be realized by any hopeful parents until they have felt it for themselves. Later, however, Charles Arthur would be born on May 13, 2001. And, on November 21, 2002, George Terrence II was born.

Our baby miracle is about love, communication, faith, devotion, and patience. From despair to indescribable delight, our love for each other and our knowing in our souls that God would make it possible gave us our longed-for miracle of parenthood.

Believe in miracles! They happen every day.

*E*arly in 2000, an astonishing photograph circulated on the Internet with an accompanying caption that identified the picture as having been taken during a surgery on a twenty-one-week-old fetus—and the fetus was holding the doctor's hand.

The photograph seemed too remarkable to be true, and many who received it in their e-mail assumed that it had to be one of those e-rumors, an urban legend, a hoax created by some Internet mischief-maker.

However, as incredible as it may seem to many of

those who have seen the inspiring photograph, it is no fanciful e-rumor or cleverly hoaxed mockup. The photograph was taken by Michael Clancy during fetal surgery being performed by Dr. Joseph Bruner on Samuel Armas, the unborn son of Julie and Alex Armas. According to Clancy, who owns the copyright on the picture, as he witnessed the procedure to correct spina bifida, he had seen the uterus shake and the baby's hand emerge from the surgical opening. Clancy said that Dr. Bruner put his finger into the baby's hand, and the baby squeezed the finger.

The dramatic impact of Clancy's photograph of that miraculous moment was labeled by many as the "Hand of Hope," and some viewers suggested that the hand of little Samuel Alexander Armas had reached out to grasp Dr. Bruner's finger, as if to thank the surgeon for granting him the gift of life.

Samuel's mother, Julie Armas, was an obstetrics nurse in Atlanta, who learned that her unborn son was diagnosed with spina bifida, a serious condition in which a baby's spine does not close properly during development. She knew that her baby would not survive if he were to be removed from her womb for any surgical procedure, but she was also aware of the remarkable work of Dr. Joseph Bruner of Vanderbilt University in Nashville. Dr. Bruner has been internationally acclaimed for performing special operations on fetuses afflicted with spina bifida while they were still in their mothers' wombs. The surgical procedure involves the medical team's removing the uterus and making a small incision to operate on the baby. Dr. Bruner acknowledged that the procedure with a fetus as young as twenty-one weeks has its risks, because if anything should go wrong, the baby would not be able to survive on its own.

Although touched by the various accounts of the incident that described little Samuel's tiny hand reaching out to grab his finger, in an article in *USA Today* (May 2, 2000), Dr. Bruner commented that both the mother and the baby were under anesthesia and could not move. During the surgery when Samuel's hand suddenly emerged from the uterus, Dr. Bruner said that he instinctively offered his finger for the baby to hold. The little hand did not squeeze his finger, but merely rested upon it.

The fact that surgery on the twenty-one-week-old fetus was successful was miracle enough for Julie and Alex Armas — with or without the optional dramatic moment of the finger squeeze. Samuel was born on or about December 2, 1999, and, according to his parents, was developing well.

*T*here is no question in the minds of John and Traci Jensen that little two-year-old Barry saved the life of his identical twin, Terry, from drowning just a few days before Thanksgiving in 2000.

The Jensens, who live in Phoenix, Arizona, had experienced a number of rather unusual occurrences that led them to believe that their twin sons were linked mentally through some psychic bond. The events of that November afternoon proved what they had long suspected: Barry and Terry could sense each other's thoughts and feelings. Each could see or feel what was happening to the other even when they weren't together.

John Jensen recalled that just before the near-fatal incident he had been reading a book, waiting for Traci to get out of the shower so they could drive across the city and visit his parents in Mesa.

"Barry was playing with a little toy truck, crawling around my chair, making appropriate motor-type sound effects with his mouth," John told us. "All of sudden, he made a strange kind of gurgling cry and started saying over and over, 'Frogie in pool . . . Frogie in pool!'"

John explained that in the weird little world that Barry and Terry shared as identical twins, their name for each other, individually and collectively, was "Frogie." Although the boys identified themselves by their given names of Barry and Terry when asked by strangers who might approach the family in supermarkets and malls and ask the names of the cute twins, when they spoke to each other they referred to themselves by the strange name of "Frogie." Traci and John had become used to the twins saying that "Frogie want eat" when they were hungry or "Frogie ca-ca" when they needed to go to the potty seat.

"At first I thought that Barry was begging to go into the pool," John said. "The boys loved to be in the water, and Traci and I would each hold one of them in our arms and move around the pool as if they were swimming. Eventually, of course, they would swim on their own, but that hadn't happened quite yet. Therefore, we kept the gate to the pool closed at all times in order to guard against either or both of the twins entering the water unsupervised.

"Earlier that morning, the boys had asked to go swimming and I had told them that it was too chilly that day to go in the water. Plus, I had explained, we were going to see Grandma and Grandpa in Mesa that afternoon and there wouldn't be time to take even a quick dip."

Barry began to thrash his arms in the air around him, and he raised his voice to a scream: "Frogie in pool! Frogie . . . pool! Help! Help!"

Suddenly John realized that Barry wasn't asking to go swimming at all. "Barry was somehow sensing that Terry had opened the gate and was in the pool," John said. "And Barry was seeing that Terry was in big trouble."

John admitted that he had become so involved in his novel that he hadn't noticed that Terry had slipped out of the room. Perhaps because Terry was three minutes older than Barry, he seemed always to be a bit more daring—and a bit more disobedient. This time Terry appeared to have asserted his two-year-old independence and gone to the pool by himself, and Barry had picked up an impression that his twin was in danger.

John yelled at Traci to get out of the shower, then he ran outside to check the pool.

"I was horrified to see little Terry floating facedown in the water," he said. "Every parent's worst nightmare is to come upon one of their children lying dead or dying. And I didn't know which was the case when I jumped in the pool and pulled Terry out of the water."

Traci stood at poolside, a robe wrapped hastily around her body, her wet hair hanging in matted strands. Crying in fear and disbelief, she reached out to take their little boy, cold and blue, from John's hands into her arms.

"When I pulled him from the water, I could feel that Terry was still breathing," John said. "I thank God that he was still alive, that we still had a chance to save him. Barry stood beside his mother, tears streaming down his face, crying over and over, 'Frogie . . . Frogie all right now.'"

As Traci was turning Terry over, he began to cough up water, and John ran, soaking wet, into the house to call 911, praying that Barry's sixth sense was accurate when he said that "Frogie" was going to be all right.

Traci continued to cradle Terry until the paramedics arrived.

"The paramedics gave Terry some oxygen, then loaded him into an ambulance to take him to the hospital," John said. "After he was given more oxygen and a doctor at the emergency room had examined him, we were able to take him home with us. Traci sat beside the boys in their infant seats in the back, and we heard Barry solemnly intone, 'Frogie bad boy.' Terry nodded his head and echoed, 'Frogie bad boy!'"

Traci reached over, hugged both of the twins, and pronounced with loving emphasis, "God loves Frogie! But Frogie very, very lucky."

Of course the Jensens knew that there had been no luck involved in Terry's narrow brush with drowning. They understood that somehow the mind-link between their two-year-old twins had saved Terry's life.

"In a way that neither Traci nor myself could fully comprehend, Barry had managed to obtain a mental image that his brother had disobeyed the family rule about never entering the pool alone and had opened the gate and jumped into the water. Since Terry couldn't swim, he had quite likely sunk like a rock. Barry playing with his truck beside my chair, had somehow seen or felt his twin struggling in the pool and alerted us to the danger."

The Jensens knew that they had an extra special reason to give thanks that Thanksgiving holiday.

And they also knew that it was time to put a lock on the pool gate.

*S*ometimes a miracle in the making can just reach out and pull someone into its energy when they least expect it.

While working as a writer for a well-known advertising agency in Virginia, Sherry Hansen Steiger was responsible for coming up with creative concepts for ad campaigns and promotions, as well as being responsible for the scripting and often the execution of these ads in the print, radio, and television media. There was always the pressure of deadlines and important meetings with clients or potential clients in a highly competitive market—and it was imperative that she be there on time that morning when an especially critical briefing with the staff was scheduled.

After taking her young daughter, Melissa, to school, Sherry headed for the expressway for what would be a forty-five-minute to an hour commute. But just before she was to make the turn onto the route that led to the expressway entrance, she had a most remarkable vision that caused her to alter her course.

What Sherry saw in her mind's eye was a vivid scene of a terrible car accident—either her own or someone else's. In either case, it dissolved the worry of being tardy to work. With the uneasy feeling in the pit of her stomach and its accompanying nausea, she was praying what she saw was merely a cautionary picture—warning her to be extra careful driving in order to avoid a potential accident.

Suddenly Sherry heard a voice in her head, nearly screaming at her to "turn right"—the *opposite* direction from the route she normally took and a turn that would take her way out of the way. In fact, it could mean an extra hour or so of driving. Once again she saw the image of a single car accident, so, trusting her instinct, she obeyed the message and turned right.

About six blocks after the turn, she heard another message telling her to "turn left." Although she knew that this was a seldom traveled road that would take her far out of her way, she once again obeyed the inner command. She had not driven far when she came upon a car upside down in the middle of the road—exactly like the picture in the vision she had been shown.

Sherry parked her car and ran to the aid of the occupants who were trapped inside. Pounding on the windows in the back of the upside-down vehicle were two small boys, one of whom was approximately three or four years old and the other was just a baby, about a year old. With tears streaming down their panic-stricken faces, they screamed to get out of the car.

Sherry saw that their mother was trapped in the driver's seat of the car. Blood streamed down the woman's face, neck, head, and arms. Sherry could see that the mother was either unconscious—or worse—so she concentrated on getting the boys out first.

It was the late 1970s, when most car models did not have power windows, and in this case it was a good thing, for the lack of an automatic mechanism allowed the windows to be individually controlled without a lock or power. Unable to get the car doors open, Sherry attempted to tell the boys to roll down the window. When shouting simple directions to the older boy didn't seem to be working, Sherry started motioning with a rolling down action of her arm and wrist and pointing in the direction of the car window handle.

Finally the boy seemed to understand, and once he had cranked the window down far enough, Sherry was able to reach in and roll it down far enough to pull the two children out of the car. While she carried the younger boy, Sherry held the big brother's hand and led them to a distance she thought safe enough should the car burst into flames.

Still hysterically crying for their mother, the boys managed to tell Sherry that their names were Alan and Jamie. Sherry told them to hold onto each other and made them promise not to move while she tried to get their mother out. Once back at the car, it became obvious that the mom wasn't able to respond, and Sherry was not capable of getting the doors open, no matter how hard she tried.

It seemed to Sherry that her only viable option would be to crawl in the window from which she had pulled the boys from the car and try to get to the mother, who was still slumped over the steering wheel unconscious. Just as Sherry was about to attempt crawling in the window, she saw a car pull over on the opposite side of the street.

Yelling for help, Sherry asked the person in the car to find a phone and call for help. Again, in those days, there were no cellular or mobile car phones to make dialing 911 an easy matter.

Back at the upside-down automobile, Sherry was excited and pleased to see that the mother had begun to move a little. The woman lifted her head slightly, and Sherry asked if she could move her arms or legs and if she could move enough so Sherry could attempt to help her out of the car. The woman seemed unable to determine where she was hurt, much less try to get out of the car. Nor did she appear to comprehend that she had been in an auto accident.

Sherry headed back toward Alan and Jamie, struggling with a sad feeling of helplessness. Then suddenly the air was filled with a loud roar and the whirling of the sounds of sirens approaching the scene of the accident.

The boys ran toward Sherry, and they both grabbed onto her and clung tightly. Sherry picked up Jamie, and from that second on, it was as if he was glued to her. Alan also held onto her skirt and would have been in her arms if she had been able to hold both of them.

"These your kids?" asked the first police officer on the scene.

Sherry explained that she was first on the scene and didn't see another car that might have been involved and had no idea how the accident occurred. All she knew when she got there was that the car was alone and upside down, the wheels still spinning and the motor still running. As she told how she managed to get the little boys out of the car, the fire trucks and ambulances arrived, and rescue workers were shouting that the car might burst into flames at any second. They were desperately trying to get the mother out of the car, and they ordered the gathering crowd to move away in case the automobile should explode.

When one of the ambulance attendants asked if the boys were injured, Alan and Jamie clutched tighter than ever to Sherry. The boys wouldn't answer the paramedic's questions, but hid their faces in Sherry's skirt and jacket.

The attendant nodded to Sherry and told her that they would take the boys to the hospital and run tests to be safe, indicating that Sherry could leave.

But Alan and Jamie wouldn't have it. They wouldn't let go of Sherry, so she volunteered to go in the ambulance with them. That was the only way the boys would go. With Sherry carrying Jamie in her arms and with Alan holding to her skirt, they all climbed in an emergency vehicle.

At the hospital, the boys wouldn't let Sherry out of their sight, so she stayed with them through the entire process of emergency care. At the same time that the boys were being examined, one of the rescue workers tried to get as much information as possible from Alan regarding the name of his father or another family member to contact.

Any attempt by a nurse or doctor to take Jamie only set him screaming. He would only stay with Sherry.

Suddenly a different kind of panic hit Sherry when she noted the time on a large wall clock that came into focus. She was now hours late for work—and no one at the office knew why or where she was. Thankfully, although obviously they were frightened, neither child seemed to be seriously hurt, so Sherry went to a pay phone to call her boss.

Sherry explained about the accident that she had come upon and that she didn't know when she would be able to leave the hospital because of the little boys' dependency on her. Also, she couldn't leave until she had knowledge of the condition of the mother and whether or not anyone would be notified to come to comfort the boys and to stay with them through the next stages of testing.

Sherry was extremely disappointed when the boss's response was: "Great. So you rescued the kids. Now get back to the office and get to work!" Although the words sounded very much like an if-you-want-to-keep-your-job threat, Sherry couldn't leave the boys.

From hospital personnel, Sherry learned that the car had burst into flames, but rescue workers had been able to get the mother out just in the nick of time. Although her condition was listed as serious, it was believed that she would recover.

It was several hours later before hospital officials managed to locate someone from the information they collected from the purse of the mother. The father arrived about 4:00 P.M.—and it was not until then that Sherry was able to loosen the grip of the two little boys as they ran into their father's arms.

Sherry arrived at her desk to be met with a series of unending questions about what had occurred from the other members of the agency. Although they were hours off-schedule, Sherry promised her boss that the project would be finished in time.

While she was answering all the questions from her fellow workers, it suddenly impacted Sherry how truly amazing the whole event was. The vision that she had seen had been a miraculous intervention so powerful that she couldn't ignore it—and it may have just saved the life of a baby, his brother, and his mother.

When Craig Green was six months old, he was slowly dying because he could not retain any food. Because of some malady, which the doctors in 1933 were unable to diagnose, he weighed less than he had at birth.

Although the Green family physician and medical experts in Albany, New York, had spent long hours with the infant, they were unable to determine either the cause or the remedy for baby Craig's rapidly deteriorating condition.

One night Sarah Green, Craig's sorrowing mother,

looked toward a window in the bedroom and saw an angel robed in white coming through the screen.

"Be not afraid," the angel said in a gentle voice. "I have come to help you. Your baby is dying; but if you heed what I tell you, he will soon be well."

As the astonished mother listened, the supernatural visitor advised her to prepare the baby's formula according to a heavenly prescription. After listing a number of ingredients that seemed an unusual mix, but were available in her own kitchen, the angel told her to blend them all together with whole milk.

"Add a little cream and beat an egg into the milk," the spiritual being said. "Your baby will be able to keep this down."

The heavenly being walked to the crib where the child lay sleeping. "Behold your son," the angel said, smiling. "He sleeps peacefully."

Tears coursed down Sarah's cheeks. "But the doctors say that little Craig will soon sleep in death," she said, barely managing to force the words past her sorrow.

The angel turned to her and spoke in a stern, authoritative manner: "Cease your weeping. Make the formula as I have given it to you, and your boy will live to be a fine man.

"Now you will lie down," the angel seemed to add as a secondary command. "You will sleep long and peacefully. I bid you farewell."

Before the young mother's startled eyes, the angel floated through the screened window and disappeared.

When the doctor called the next day, Sarah decided not to tell him of the angelic visitation. But she did ask about the odd formula that the heavenly being had prescribed for her baby.

The doctor heard her out before he responded. "Well, under ordinary circumstances and conditions, I would feel that a change of diet might be harmful, especially with some of the ingredients that you listed. But. . . ."

Before he completed his reply the doctor hesitated several seconds. "But I must be honest with you, Mrs. Green. Little Craig seems to be walking in the shadow of death. You might as well try the new formula. You have nothing to lose."

Since Craig Green is over seventy years old, there remains no question that the angel-prescribed formula worked for him.

"Mother told me how she knelt in prayer to God and thanked him for sending the angel to save her baby," Green told us. "The change in formula might well have been the sole cause of my survival, but I have often felt that there was much more to the angel's visitation than that.

"As I heard Mother telling the story again and again to family and friends over the years," he continued, "I have developed my own theory that the peculiar mix of baby formula with some strange, but ordinary, additions—a pinch of cinnamon, a bit of garlic powder, and other seemingly unusual elements—was only a diversion. I believe that the heavenly formula the angel provided was only a kind of physical stimulus that encouraged hope in my mother's heart. In other words, instead of standing by helplessly watching her baby die, she could actually do something to cure him.

"In my opinion," Craig Green concluded, "The angel exerted a great deal of healing energy as it approached my crib and that the change in formula may have been only incidental to my rapid recovery."

*T*wo tiny little lives made their earthly appearance twelve weeks before their due date, and in all likelihood, they and their worried parents were hardly aware of how famous they were about to become. Not only would a photo of the frail twin girls gain worldwide attention, but the girls would set a precedent that very likely would save the lives of many other preemies through an innocent display of affection—one for the other—as the two made national headlines in newspapers throughout the world.

Kyrie and Brielle Jackson were born October 17,

1995, to Heidi and Paul Jackson at Memorial Hospital in Worcester, Massachusetts. Their little bodies were so small and underdeveloped that their very survival was tenuous at best, with Kyrie weighing in at a mere two pounds three ounces and Brielle at a mere two pounds.

Premature babies born this early and at such a low weight face difficult odds: The trauma of birth before their time forces their entire system into action when the organs are not yet fully formed and cannot adequately perform their intricate functions. Often incapable of supporting life if left to their own resources, the stresses on the miniature heart, lungs, and kidneys can prove too burdensome to sustain, and, one by one, they simply shut down. Even though in recent years highly sophisticated technical equipment paired with superb medical training and care boosts the chance of survival by a large percentage, many cases still boil down to faith and prayer and a power far greater than our modern technology.

As soon as the twin girls were born, it was obvious they would need all the assistance of the best available care. They were each put into an individual incubator— a routine practice thought to reduce the chance of infection and increase the monitoring capabilities for the good of each infant. Placed in the neonatal intensive care unit at the Medical Center of Central Massachusetts, surprisingly, the girls held their own, although struggling to survive.

Little Kyrie slowly but steadily gained in weight and strength, but for some reason, Brielle did not improve. Immediately, she was put on a respirator to reduce the burden on her lungs. This helped temporarily.

Brielle began to exhibit a growing discomfort that soon mounted to incessant crying that holding and feeding and other comforts would not appease. She seemed to be having trouble breathing and although the nurse tried many things, including aspirating Brielle's breathing passages and increasing the flow of oxygen to her incubator, nothing seemed to be working. Suddenly her vital functions took a dive.

Brielle, gasping for air, began to turn blue. Her heart rate was erratic. The girls' parents, Heidi and Paul, helplessly stood by as Brielle's prospects for survival shrank before their very eyes. Perhaps it was good fortune or destiny that sparked a thought in Gayle Kasparian, the attending nurse. Nurse Kasparian remembered hearing of an innovative technique for treating premature babies. A colleague had told her about *double-bedding*, as it was called, which had been tried in Europe, but had never been tried in the United States. The method consisted simply of putting multiple births, especially premature ones, together in the same bed.

The Jacksons eagerly gave their permission to try double-bedding. So in desperation, the quick-thinking, kindhearted nurse picked up Brielle and put her into the incubator next to her twin sister, Kyrie, whom she had not physically been near since their birth. The nurse had no sooner closed the door to the incubator when they all witnessed the girls moving toward one another in a cuddling manner. Amazingly, within seconds Kyrie reached out her little bitty arm and wrapped it around Brielle's shoulders as if to welcome her back to a state of togetherness that should never have been interrupted.

Miraculously, Kyrie's comforting touch was the saving grace that turned Brielle's condition around. Fussy, weakened, and deteriorating Brielle instantly calmed down and her vital signs returned to normal almost immediately! It was as though the touch and love that bonded the twins together in the first place had healed her.

So astounding was this radical physical turnaround and the changes in vitals so dramatic, that at first nurse Kasparian could hardly believe her eyes. She wondered if the medical equipment providing the readout of Brielle's heart rate, blood-oxygen, and other vitals could be faulty, but seeing how peaceful Brielle now appeared gave further proof that something else was at work.

Heidi and Paul Jackson could only burst into tears

of joy as they experienced an overwhelming thankfulness that filled their hearts at the healing embrace of their infant daughters. The rhythmic beat of both teeny little hearts of their beloved miracle twins must have been music to their ears and eyes as they, too, witnessed the synchronized measurements—now stable and vital.

The equipment was indeed accurate. Little Brielle promptly fell asleep, wrapped in the arms of her twin. In the comfort of her sister's presence, Brielle rebounded. From that moment on, she gained in strength and weight, pulling through the crisis. Kyrie was the medicine Brielle needed, as they continued to sleep side by side, arm in arm.

Chris Christo, then a photographer for the *Worcester Telegram & Gazette,* captured the moment of the twins' embrace, as the preemies made history at Memorial Hospital as the first U.S. double-bedding. The article and photo were entitled "The Rescuing Hug," and the touching story and picture soon gained notoriety. Appearing in *Life* magazine and *Reader's Digest,* the photo eventually found its way to the Internet as this picture truly is worth a thousand words.

A much relieved Heidi and Paul Jackson took their beautiful daughters home just before Christmas, when they were a little over two months old. The barely there two-pound preemies were now just over five pounds each, but healthy enough to leave hospital care. They were the best Christmas present imaginable to their parents. At home, the girls continued their togetherness, sleeping in the same crib—happily growing and thriving.

An interesting irony is that nurse Gayle Kasparian was concerned that her decision to break protocol and place the premature twins in the same incubator might end up getting her in trouble—regardless of the successful outcome. Gayle Kasparian even wondered if she might lose her job when her boss learned of the incident. Kasparian's nurse manager, Susan Fitzback, would normally have had to give her approval for anything this unorthodox, but she was out of town at a conference. Fitzback was due back the very day after Brielle and Kyrie Jackson had been placed together in this manner.

Intriguingly, as fact is often stranger than fiction, the conference she was attending was about *double-bedding*! Linda M. Lutes gave a presentation at the conference, on double-bedding. Linda M. Lutes, of the Oklahoma Infant Transition Program, an affiliate of Oklahoma University, was the colleague that Kasparian first heard of the procedure from—at a conference—a year earlier. So, of course, when Susan Fitzback returned, she was fired up and hoping to implement this method.

In making her rounds as usual, another nurse

pointed out to Fitzback how sweet the two preemies looked who were nestled together—as she pointed to the incubator housing Brielle and Kyrie. Word had spread throughout the hospital and many of the employees and visitors wended their way up to peek in the infant nursery window to view the teensy adorable cuddling babies. Fitzback was so surprised and pleased that she gave the nurse who had just directed her to the sight a hug right on the spot, as she expressed how beautiful she found that sight to be. And the hospital has approved the method ever since.

Since Brielle Jackson's remarkable recovery, *double-bedding*, or *co-bedding* as it is sometimes called, has been tried at other hospitals around the country—and with great success. Scientific research at hospitals, schools, and institutions continues to investigate the validity of the method.

So far, the research indicates that co-bedded infants do in fact develop at a faster rate. They have better feeding patterns and, in general, better vital signs. The inability of undeveloped lungs in premature babies to function properly often results in breathing problems and even the cessation of breathing altogether. But, in co-bedding, it seems that even simple movement or squirming by one baby can stimulate the other into taking a breath; co-bedding babies spend less time on oxygen. The overall effects are sufficient to decrease the average length of time a premature baby has to stay in the hospital in special care, which also adds the benefits of being cost effective and more efficient.

The Jacksons, however, don't need the research results. When it came to the point where the best of equipment was not working and Brielle was not expected to live, the miracle of a risk-taking nurse, a rescuing hug, and continuing cuddling between siblings gave proof enough—it worked for them.

Perhaps it might also serve as a reminder to all of us to embrace those we love more often on a regular basis and of the healing power of a hug!

When Robert Kosolofski left for his job at the dairy at 2:30 A.M. the morning of February 23, 1994, he had no idea that his two-year-old daughter Karlee had tried to follow him out to the garage. If he had caught sight of the toddler in her pajamas and diapers leaving the house, he surely would have stopped and carried her back to bed. There was a windchill factor of forty degrees below zero that morning.

As the Kosolofskis re-created the near-fatal events, it appeared that little Karlee had pulled on a coat and a pair of boots over her pajamas and set out to go with her daddy to work at the local dairy in Roleau, Saskatchewan. When she pushed open the door to go outside, it slammed shut behind her and locked automatically. Doctors later estimated that Karlee had frozen within minutes of exposure to the forty-below temperature.

When Karlee's mother, Karrie Kosolofski, awakened around 8:00 A.M., she was startled to discover that her two-year-old baby was not in her bed. After searching the house without finding Karlee—and noticing that her coat and boots were missing—Karrie began to fear the worst. It seemed impossible that Karlee would have gone outside, but when Karrie opened the door to check, she found their only child frozen stiff on the doorstep.

By the time the ambulance got Karrie and her daughter to the hospital, little Karlee had no pulse and no heartbeat. Dr. John Burgess, a cardiovascular and thoracic surgeon at Plains Health Center in Regina, told reporters that Karlee had literally been frozen like a block of ice. Her body temperature had dropped from a normal 98.6 to 57.2 degrees. From the descriptions given by the attending physicians at the Health Center, one can visualize poor little Karlee's tiny legs so frozen and rigid, so delicately fragile, that they appeared as though they could easily snap right off, like icicles.

A dedicated medical team began working desperately to bring the two-year-old girl back to life. Doctors connected her to a heart-and-lung machine, which, for nearly five hours, slowly withdrew Karlee's blood, warmed it, then recirculated it into her body.

Her heart began to beat again when her body temperature reached 77 degrees. Doctors shocked Karlee's heart twice to keep it beating until her tiny body gradually warmed up to 98.6 degrees.

Remarkably, none of Karlee's vital organs, including her brain, were damaged, because, according to the doctors, she had frozen so quickly. The only lasting damage sustained by the little girl was the loss of the lower part of her left leg due to frostbite.

Dr. Joy Dobson, an anesthesiologist at Plains Health Center, declared that they had all witnessed a miracle when a baby frozen like a block of ice had been brought back to life.

According to *The Guinness Book of Records*, Karlee Kosolofski's icy temperature of 57.2 degrees was seven degrees lower than the lowest body temperature that anyone had ever survived.

On February 24, 2001, thirteen-month-old Erika, clad only in her diaper, wandered away from the home where she had been sleeping with her mother, Leyla Nordby, and her two-year-old sister and was found outside at 3:00 A.M. in subzero weather.

When her mother discovered Erika's frozen little body and called for help, the paramedics found the infant's toes frozen together and her mouth frozen shut, thereby preventing them from inserting a breathing tube into her throat.

Leyla had no idea how her thirteen-month-old daughter could have managed to walk outside on a night when the temperature dipped to twenty degrees below zero. Leyla and her two daughters had been overnight guests at a friend's house. Leyla and her friend had hired a baby-sitter to look after their children, and the two women had gone out socializing. They returned home around 10:30 P.M., paid and released the baby-sitter, and everybody had gone to bed.

At around 3:00 A.M., Leyla awakened and discovered that her baby was not in bed with her. After searching the house and still not finding the infant, someone noticed that the door appeared not to have latched properly when the baby-sitter left. A few minutes later, a frantic Leyla found Erika facedown in the snow, her little hands curled beneath her body, with only a diaper to provide any kind of covering against the subzero weather.

Doctors at Stollery Children's Hospital in Edmonton, British Columbia, said that when she was brought in for attention, the baby's heart had stopped beating and her body temperature was 60.8 degrees. A medical team set up a heart-and-lung machine to begin warming the little girl's body, but before they could begin the procedure, her heart began beating on its own.

Dr. Alf Conradi, director of the pediatric intensive care unit at Stollery Children's Hospital, told the press on February 26 that the thirteen-month-old baby was doing well. While her frostbite injuries were considerable, she appeared not to have suffered any permanent organ or brain damage.

Dr. Allen De Caen, a pediatric intensive care specialist at the hospital, said that he felt humbled by the little girl's incredible recovery. He expressed his opinion that one could fairly use the word *miracle* in describing the baby's dramatic survival.

*T*hirty-four-year-old Carla Sanden had told her husband, Virgil, that she planned to work at her job as a nurse until the baby came. But that late afternoon in May 2001, she wasn't so certain that she could make good on her intentions. She was nearly eight months pregnant, and she had gained a lot more weight than she had believed possible. She had overheard a couple of her fellow nurses referring to her as "Moby Dick, the great white whale."

As she lay down on the sofa in their living room and swung her throbbing feet off the floor, she felt as though there were few areas in her body that didn't ache. She had worked at the clinic in a suburb of Laramie, Wyoming, ever since Virgil got out of the service in 1997. A Wisconsin girl, she had fallen in love with the cute Marine from Wyoming when they met during a vacation in San Diego in 1992. After a long-distance romance, a whirlwind courtship, and a few years of living on a military base, they had moved back to Virgil's hometown where he took over his uncle's hardware store and lumber yard. Carla and Virgil had endured some hard times, given birth to two rambunctious kids—a six-year-old boy and a four-year-old girl—got pregnant again, and still loved each other.

"I was hoping to catch a few winks before making supper," she told us. "We live about four miles out in the country, so it is usually nice and quiet in the late afternoon. The kids were out playing in the yard, so I really wanted to take advantage of the peace and quiet. I put some soothing music on the CD player and closed my eyes."

Carla had been asleep for only a few minutes when a loud noise outside jolted her awake. At almost the same time, her son Keith ran into the house and shouted that a car had gone off the road, ran into the ditch, and burst into flames.

"Mom," he screamed, "there's a lady and two little

kids in the car."

Carla called 911, but she knew that she would have to do something to help the woman and her children trapped in the burning car until the fire truck and rescue team got there.

With a great effort of will and with Keith tugging at her arm to help, she managed to get off the sofa, wishing anew that she hadn't gained so much weight with the pregnancy.

When she walked outside, she felt her stomach lurch with panic. The car had gone off the road, into the ditch, struck a fence post, and, as Keith had informed her, burst into flames. Her four-year-old daughter, Krista, was sitting on a swing, clutching the ropes to the seat, sobbing loudly in fear.

Carla could see two small children in the back window, pounding on the glass—and she could hear their terrible screams. Their mother appeared to be slumped unconscious on the steering wheel of the crashed and burning vehicle.

Carla knew that she had to do something. Right away.

"Mom, stay away from the car. It might explode!" Keith shouted at her as she walked toward the flames. "I don't want you to die, Mom! Stop!"

Carla picked up the baseball bat that leaned against a

wall of the garage. Most nights when Virgil first got home, he liked to hit a few pop-ups for Keith to catch. This afternoon, Carla would have another use for the hardwood bat.

As quickly as she could, Carla walked to the back window of the car and swung at it with all her strength. "My added bulk may have helped me in this case," she said, "for the back window caved in after only a couple of hits."

The flames were unbearably hot, but Carla reached in and pulled a little girl, not more than two years old, out of the backseat. "I set her on the ground, and she ran, coughing, toward Keith, who was still standing on the road and screaming at me to get away from the burning car."

A boy, probably four or so, was tugging at his mother, who, praise God, Carla saw had regained consciousness.

"Crawl out the back!" Carla yelled at the woman. "Hurry! The car's about to blow up!"

Although the woman was bleeding from a head wound and was terribly burned on her legs and lower body, she somehow managed to get far enough into the backseat for Carla to grasp her hand.

"Thank God, the fire and rescue crew arrived just then, and two husky firemen pulled the woman and her four-year-old son free of the burning car," Carla said. "They sprayed the car with some foam and pretty much extinguished the flames in a matter of minutes. The paramedics got right at looking after the woman and her children, and I knew my work was finished."

Carla felt her legs go out from under her as she was walking with Keith and Krista toward the house. Paramedics ran to check on her, asking if she was hurt.

"Nope," she told them. "Just pooped and pregnant!"

Carla brushed aside talk of her being a hero. She protested that she was a nurse, just doing what she had been trained to do: Help people whenever and wherever the need arose. She did like the way Virgil fussed over her when he got home, though.

Carla said that the mother of the two children suffered very severe burns and had to spend considerable time in intensive care in the hospital's burn wing. The four-year-old was also quite badly burned and had a couple of broken ribs from the force of the crash against the strap on his car seat. The little girl had only minor bruises and scratches.

Carla said that her own baby, another boy, Karl, was born without incident on June 18. The grateful husband and father of the crash victims sent her six dozen roses when she was in the hospital after giving birth.

"*For* thirty years now, people have been telling me that what I experienced must have been a dream," Pauline, an elementary school teacher from Idaho, told us. "But I will always believe that the healing of my two-year-old baby sister was a true miracle from Jesus."

In 1970, when Pauline was five years old, she lived in a rural area of Idaho and shared a room with her sisters Jolene and Gloria. Little Gloria, who at the time was only nineteen months old, had become very ill with pneumonia and was running a high fever. Before their mother,

Maxine, left to work at the restaurant in town, she told the older girls that they must take turns placing damp cloths on Gloria's forehead to help keep the fever down.

"Although in retrospect this responsibility appointed to us by our mother seems ill-suited and above the reach of two little girls, Mom certainly couldn't have afforded to hire anyone else to take care of little Gloria," Pauline said. "Mom was only thirty years old at that time, and she was left widowed with three little girls to take care of when our father was killed in a farm accident in the fall of 1969. Waitressing in the nearby small town didn't pay Mom much, and there were few big tippers among the farmers who patronized the place, most of whom were scraping hard to make their own ends meet. Mom had no money to spare to hire a baby-sitter to look after little Gloria, so that left my big sister Jolene, who was eight, and my five-year-old self to be little nurses."

Pauline remembered that after their mother had left for work, Jolene put her head to Gloria's chest and said that she could hear a rattling sound when the baby breathed.

"She looked up with sad eyes and said that little Gloria was going to die," Pauline remembered. "When you are barely five and your big sister speaks with such authority, you get really frightened. I started to cry, believing that our baby sister was truly dying. And, perhaps, for all intents and purposes, she was."

Their mother had taken Gloria to the doctor that afternoon, and he had given her a prescription for some medicine to help clear up the congestion and to allow the baby to breathe easier.

"Mom didn't have enough money to pay for the full prescription, but the pharmacist had agreed to give her a small bottle of cough medicine and the pills the doctor had prescribed if she promised to come back in a week and pay the rest of the amount," Pauline said.

"Before she left for work, Mom had given us exact instructions about when to give Gloria the pills. She warned us that the baby might try to spit out the bitter-tasting pills, so we were to dip them in some honey before we tried to give them to her."

Pauline watched Jolene carefully move the pill in the honeycomb without getting any wax on the tiny bit of medicine.

"Jolene had always had these long, graceful fingers," Pauline said, "and she put the pill in Gloria's mouth like an expert doctor. Gloria liked the honey, and the pill dissolved fast while she licked it. While Gloria was still smacking her lips, Jolene asked me to sing or hum to help the baby fall asleep. Although Jolene kind of bossed me around in some ways, she always said that I could keep a tune and sing better than she could."

Pauline remembered that both Jolene and Gloria fell asleep while she was singing.

"I pulled a blanket over Jolene and kissed her on the forehead," she said, "then I did the same for Gloria in her crib. Next, I got down on my knees to say my bedtime prayers. I asked Jesus over and over to please heal my little sister."

Pauline finished her bedtime prayers, and she clearly remembers wondering if Jesus was really listening and, most of all, if Jesus really cared for little Gloria or for any of their family. She fell asleep, worrying about the place that she, her sisters, and her mother might have in Jesus' heart.

"Later, I was awakened by someone calling my name," Pauline said. "I will swear to my dying day that I was fully awake when I turned over and clearly saw Jesus and an angel standing beside the bed. Jolene always clicked on our Cinderella nightlight, and I could distinctly see these two majestic figures in our little room, standing in the soft glow of that light."

Pauline said that Jesus smiled at her, then beckoned for the angel to step closer to the bedside. The angel was dressed in really bright white robes, and he (or she) had a very full set of wings. When the heavenly being drew nearer, Pauline saw that he held a large book in his hands.

Jesus nodded at the angel, and the heavenly being

took a feather pen from behind his ear and pointed with its tip at something he had written in the book.

"I leaned forward and saw that he had written my mom's name, Jolene's name, my name—and *little Gloria's name*," Pauline said. "I knew that meant that Gloria was going to live! The angel smiled at me, looked up at Jesus—and they both disappeared."

Pauline understood that Jesus had shown her that her family did matter to him and that their names were recorded in His big Book of Life. "And the fact that Gloria's name was written there meant that she was going to get better," she said. "I knew then that she wouldn't die of pneumonia, that she had been healed by Jesus and the angel."

Pauline shook Jolene awake and told her that Jesus and an angel had just appeared in their bedroom to heal Gloria.

"Jolene didn't seem to hear what I had said," Pauline recalled. "I guess she thought I was waking her up to put a cool cloth on Gloria's forehead, for she yawned and reached for the basin and dipped a hand towel in the water. As she placed the cloth on the baby's forehead, she commented that Gloria felt cooler to her touch."

Pauline finally got Jolene to understand about the wonderful appearance of Jesus, the angel, and the Book of Life.

"Once I got her to listen to me," Pauline said, "Jolene got down on her knees beside Gloria's crib and offered up prayers of praise and thanks to Jesus."

Both the girls were awake when their mother returned from work shortly after eleven o'clock, and they told her that Gloria had been healed of her illness by Jesus and an angel.

"Mom just kind of gave us a 'that's nice' look until she picked up little Gloria and felt how much cooler she was," Pauline said. "The next day when she took her to the doctor, he told her that Gloria's lungs had somehow miraculously cleared up almost completely. She had gone from being dangerously congested to having clear lungs overnight."

While her mother and other adults told Pauline that she had experienced only a vivid dream of Jesus and an angel, everyone did acknowledge little Gloria's remarkable, unexplained overnight recovery from severe pneumonia.

"I know that Jolene believed me—and maybe our combined faiths helped to heal our baby sister," Pauline said. "Regardless of how others might consider my story, I have never forgotten what I believe to have been a true vision of belonging to Jesus, and such a belief has comforted me many times since during any difficult times on my earthly path."

Melanie Killian told us of the painful delivery that she underwent, which brought her the remarkable bonus of seeing what she believed to be the reassuring image of Jesus.

Melanie said that she knew that she would have a difficult delivery. The doctors had debated whether or not they should take the child through cesarean section, but they decided to deal with the problem of the breeched baby in the delivery room. Melanie was advised that she would be given only a mild painkiller. They could not give her a general anesthetic, because she would have to help with the birth process.

"When the dilation had neared completion, the birth agony was driving me out of my mind," Melanie continued her account of her ordeal. "And maybe that was just what happened, for I suddenly felt a weird whirling sensation—and 'pop,' I was floating over the bed in the labor room, looking down on my body and the nurse who was trying to ease my pain."

Melanie was shocked to see how contorted her facial features appeared. "At first I thought I must have died, but then my body below began to move and let out a terrible cry of pain."

Melanie was really baffled. That was definitely the Melanie Killian that she knew and loved down there on the bed, writhing in what was obviously awful agony. But it was also Melanie up near the ceiling, watching the scene below, feeling absolutely no pain at all.

"I saw the nurse measure my dilation, and tell the doctor that I was ready," she said. "When the doctor told me to push, I found myself back in the delivery room, moaning with the terrible pain. I wanted to go back up near the ceiling again where there was no pain."

Melanie did leave her body again during the delivery. "I saw my face pale and glistening with sweat. Then the baby came—a beautiful daughter, our Elise—and I saw that everything was all right."

For the first time in hours, she thought of her husband, Roger, who had been sitting anxiously in the waiting room. "Just like that," Melanie said, "I was hovering over him, wanting to tell him about our beautiful baby girl, our little Elise. But then I became aware of a strong force, tugging, pulling at me, and I seemed to be being dragged into some kind of dark, dark tunnel."

Melanie feared that she was about to make the final and ultimate trip from her physical body. "I thought, 'Oh, no! I get through the terrible agony of the delivery—and now I die!'"

She fought an awful moment of panic, and then she perceived a glowing light beginning to form in the darkness of the tunnel.

"The light began to coalesce into a human figure. I could begin to distinguish a face—eyes, mouth, nose. I thought for certain that it was my guardian angel coming to take me into the light," Melanie recalled. "But then the image became that of Jesus—or at least my idea of how Jesus looks. I may not have the standard belief of certain regular churchgoers, but I have never doubted that Jesus exists somewhere in a dimension of time and space. And now, strange as it may seem to some people, Jesus stood there before me.

"His eyes were warm and kind, and I felt an overwhelming peace permeate every aspect of my being.

His voice was soft and gentle.

"'It is not yet your time to come home, Melanie,' he told me. 'Return to your body and to your baby. Remember that Divine Love is the one great power that moves the universe. Without it, there could not exist the wonderful harmony that exists in the celestial world of the spirit. Feel my Divine Love flowing from me to your heart, mind, and soul. From this day forward, manifest the harmony of Divine Love in your thought, word, and deed and do all that you can to bring about happiness in the hearts of all those with whom you share your life.'"

Melanie saw the image of Jesus raise his hand in the universal sign of peace and farewell; and just before his form disappeared, she heard him say: "Return now, my child. Return to your Earth body feeling better, more positive, more loving than you have felt in months."

The next thing Melanie knew, she opened her eyes, and a nurse was bending over her. "Hey," the nurse smiled. "Where did you go? Did you leave us for a while?"

"I guess I really was gone for a while," Melanie concluded her account of her experience. "I was gone in a way that the nurse might not be able to imagine. But for me, I returned with a renewed spirit and a heart that was filled with rejoicing. The terrible pain of the delivery had been well worth its results: a beautiful new soul in our daughter Elise and the blessing of the Master Jesus."

*I*n 1993, when Jill Crosland of Salt Lake City, Utah, was twenty weeks pregnant, a routine utltrasound scan revealed that her unborn baby had a noncancerous tumor the size of a lemon on his tiny chest. Doctors explained that the growth of the tumor would prevent the development of the baby's lungs and cause death. They suggested that she end the pregnancy.

But Jill told reporter Steve Plamann that she just couldn't give her consent to terminate the pregnancy. She had felt little Ben moving around inside her;

she had seen him on the ultrasound sucking his thumb. Somehow she knew that she had to save him.

Jill had heard of the work of Dr. Michael Harrison, a pediatric surgeon at the University of California–San Francisco, who had performed the first successful invasive fetal surgery at UCSF in 1989. During the pioneering surgery, Dr. Harrison had corrected a congenital diaphragmatic hernia, which had been crowding the lungs of the unborn child and stunting its growth. When she contacted him in 1993, Dr. Harrison and his medical team had performed numerous successful surgeries on human fetuses.

Although Dr. Harrison agreed to perform the surgery on her unborn child, he advised Jill that Ben's chances of surviving the procedure were less than 50 percent.

Jill admitted that she was terrified, but she put her faith in God and in the skill of Dr. Harrison's surgical team.

When Jill Crosland was twenty-four weeks pregnant, she was given drugs to prevent her from going into premature labor, and Dr. Harrison began the delicate three-hour surgical procedure. First, the surgeons carefully cut open the womb to expose the fetus, which weighed only about twenty-four ounces. The baby was partially removed so Dr. Harrison could raise Ben's tiny arm, cut into his chest just below the armpit, and remove the tumor. As soon as possible after the tumor had been excised from the fetus, the surgical team quickly stitched Ben up and replaced him in the womb. The amniotic fluid that had been lost due to the surgical procedure was replaced with a warm saline solution, and Jill was sutured together again.

After the operation, Jill remembered lying in the delivery room and receiving the good news from the nurses that the procedure had been a complete success. The joyful mother was able to hear little Ben's heartbeat on the monitor, and she recalled how thrilled she had been by the rhythmic sound of life and how she had thanked God for the miracle.

Five weeks later—and ten weeks before his due date—Ben was born, weighing only three pounds, seven ounces. Although he had undergone the surgical procedure and was premature, Ben survived.

At the time that Jill gave the interview to Steve Plamann (*National Enquirer,* April 18, 1995), she was delighted to state that Ben was a healthy two-year-old. Every time she looked at her little boy, she said, she saw a living miracle.

One hot, sticky August noon Lillian Baumann was driving her three children to a park for a picnic when one of her car tires blew on a remote rural section of road in Georgia.

As she was struggling to maintain control of her automobile, Lillian's two-year-old daughter, Abby, although securely anchored in her car seat in the back-seat, smashed her upper lip against the metal picnic basket that her older brother, eight-year-old Lucas, was clutching in his arms. Ten-year-old Lindsay, beside her in the front seat, bumped her head against the door on the passenger side of the car.

When Lillian managed to halt the vehicle on a gravel shoulder of the road, she could see that Abby's lip was bleeding profusely. She knew that the wound would require stitches and that she had better get Abby to a hospital as soon as possible.

"Momma!" Abby cried, holding her tiny fingers to her lip in a futile attempt to hold back the bleeding. "Hurt. Owwie!"

Lillian knew that her baby was in pain, but she realized that little Abby was probably also as confused and frightened by the flow of blood streaming into her mouth and over her chin.

Lucas didn't help matters at all when he started yelling that Abby was going to bleed to death.

"Gross!" Lindsay pronounced in wide-eyed disgust from her position beside Lillian in the front seat.

Lillian had never changed a flat tire in her life. She thought tires weren't supposed to go flat anymore. Lucas valiantly helped her remove the jack and the spare tire from the trunk, but she was well aware that her young son had never even watched anyone change a flat.

"Lucas," she warned as he stumbled against a back door with the jack, "you're only going to hurt yourself!"

"But, Mom," he argued, "we've got to get Abby to a doctor. She is really bleeding bad!"

Lillian tried to calm herself by recalling the medical fact that head and scalp wounds always bleed heavily and appear worse than they are, but the fact remained that somehow she had to change the tire and get her baby to the emergency ward of a hospital.

Five . . . ten minutes went by. There had been no cars on the desolate road in that time. And there were no cars in sight.

The humid August heat was doing its worst to make the situation even more unbearable. Lindsay had crawled into the backseat to hold a handkerchief to Abby's wounded lip. Abby was pale, trembling, and making tiny, frightened whimpering sounds.

Lillian was quickly approaching her panic level when a smiling young man on a motor scooter appeared and offered to help.

"I would really appreciate it," Lillian freely admitted. "My baby is hurt and needs medical attention. And this heat just makes everything that much worse."

"No problem." Their rescuer smiled in an easy manner. Then, turning to Lucas, he winked and said, "You can hand me the tools when I ask for them."

The boy, who identified himself as Scooter Murphy, worked quickly, and he had the task completed in a matter of minutes.

"Wow, man," Lucas pronounced his admiration of

the older boy, "you had that fixed in no time. And you didn't even break a sweat. How can you not sweat in this heat?"

Lillian offered Scooter a cup of lemonade from their picnic thermos jug.

"Oh, no, thanks." Scooter laughed. "Never touch the stuff!"

Lillian smiled at his joke. "It's only lemonade, Scooter. You must be thirsty on such a hot day, riding your motor scooter in the blazing sun and fixing flat tires for helpless ladies and kids in distress."

"I'm all right," Scooter told her as he got on his vehicle. "You'd better hurry now and get Abby to a doctor. She is really bleeding bad."

Before he rode away, Scooter refused Lillian's offer of money for his help, saying that he no longer had need of any cash. "I won the biggest lottery you can imagine," he said as he sped off in a cloud of dust.

Later that night, however, after Abby had received stitches on her upper lip at the emergency room of the hospital and the Baumann family was home safe and sound, Lillian and her husband, Merle, felt that it would only be right to send the lad a check for his trouble. They opened the telephone directory and began calling all the Murphys in their area.

After a few calls Lillian was speaking to the mother of the teenaged Good Samaritan, who seemed very guarded in her response and rather coolly asked Lillian to describe the boy who had changed her tire.

Puzzled, Lillian obliged, right down to a description of the high school class ring Scooter was wearing.

She felt the hairs stand up on her neck when the woman's tone changed from suspicion to tears. When she regained her composure, Mrs. Murphy informed Lillian that their son, Michael, "Scooter," had been killed on that remote rural road just over a year before. He had been trying out the motor scooter that they had bought him for graduation and he had been side-swiped by a truck.

Mrs. Murphy went on to state that her son had been a good boy who always derived pleasure from helping others.

Lillian could only express her sympathy and whisper around her own tears that it would appear that Scooter was somehow still helping people whenever he could. "Today he came from Heaven to work a miracle for our family," she told Mrs. Murphy.

*E*sther Gordon told us that when complications developed during the birth of her son, she lay for a time on the delivery table, officially diagnosed as dead.

Problems arose shortly after she had been admitted to the North Dakota hospital on July 22, 1985, and unfortunately suffered a day and night of excruciating labor pains.

"The pain was so terrible that I lost consciousness several times," Esther related. "And I think the pain was made even worse by the fact that my husband, Scott, had just left for New York on a business trip. We thought that we had plenty of time for him to make a four-day trip and return home in time for the baby to come, but we had certainly been wrong. This was in the day before everyone carried cell phones with them wherever they went, and our neighbor, Pauline, said she would keep trying to leave messages and getting a hold of Scott. My parents and sister, as well as Scott's family, lived in Seattle, and my mother was making arrangements to fly out to be with me.

"When it came time for me to deliver, I was in a state of shock. I had lost touch with reality and had become unconscious."

Then, according to Esther, she was floating through space in the most beautiful place she had ever seen. She remembered feeling free and thinking what a wonderful sensation she was experiencing.

Esther recalled drifting down a long, dark tunnel that seemed to stretch ahead of her for miles and miles. Finally, she reached its end.

"There, at the end of the tunnel, I saw a baby boy, also floating in space," Esther said. "I knew the baby was my unborn son, and I tried to reach out for him. That was when I heard or felt him say inside my consciousness, 'Mommy, you have to go back so that I can be born!'"

Esther said that she continued attempting to touch him, to hold him.

"Your daddy and I want to name you Holden, after Daddy's grandfather," she said. "Please, Holden, come to me. Come to your mommy."

Later, when she was asked about her impression of the long tunnel and the effect that the sight of the baby had upon her, Esther replied that she believed that she was somewhere in the heavens and that she was dead.

"I felt absolutely and completely comfortable in that state of being," Esther said. "I think I probably felt very much like the astronauts feel when they are floating in space, but I felt terribly sad that my baby would not be born. I thought that maybe Holden and I could still be together in the afterlife, even though he had never been able to live on Earth."

Then, as Esther floated in space before the form of her son, the child somehow spoke again to her spirit being: "Mommy, I am going now to be born. They are taking me out of your body even though you are here with me. Please, please, come back and be my mommy. I love you. I need you. Don't let me be born without you!"

And then the baby seemed to be propelled through space, moving away from her at a great rate of movement.

"When I looked around to see where my son had

gone, it seemed as though I could see his little body zooming down to Earth far, far below me," Esther said. "And then I could see the hospital as if I were watching some kind of movie. Next I could see right into the delivery room, and I saw the doctor and nurses working on me."

Her doctor later told her that she had stopped breathing, and anxious medical attendants could find no heartbeat. Clinically, Esther was dead; but her doctor worked feverishly to reverse the cruel verdict. Desperately he and his staff tried every procedure they knew to bring the deceased woman back to life. They had just delivered a healthy baby son. It would be a tragedy if they were to lose the mother.

"My doctor told me that they had fought for nearly thirteen minutes to save my life," Esther said, "but all I remember is floating into eternity—and then suddenly exerting a great effort of will. I didn't want to die. I wanted to come back to Earth and be Holden's mother. I wanted to see him as a baby, as a child, as a teenager, as a grown man. I knew that I had the strength of spirit to return to my body, but I knew that I could come back only if I willed it to be so.

"When I was finally able to float out of the dark tunnel, I was in an open area with blue skies and white clouds, and everything around me was beautiful beyond description," Esther said. "When I regained complete consciousness, I was in an oxygen tent, and the nurse told me that I had given birth to a fine baby son."

Both mother and child remained for several days in the hospital, thus allowing Esther ample time to recover from the tremendous strain under which her system had been placed. It was during this time that she was informed by her physician of her technical death.

Esther Gordon stated that she considered her near-death experience to have been a "wonderful" occurrence. "I am grateful that I was given an opportunity to get a good look at the next life, but I thank God for sparing me and for letting me come back so that I could take care of my son."

*I*n August 1994, Tammy Cook's husband, Dale, and two of his coworkers from the real estate office had left on a long fishing weekend, leaving her home with their five-year-old son, Jimmy, and two-year-old son, Curtis.

At that time the Cooks lived in a duplex next to a city park with a great many trees and well-kept lawns. Tammy enjoyed strolling with the children in the park, and the first two days of her husband's absence passed without incident.

A person who lived most comfortably according to a

regular schedule, Tammy would feed the children promptly at 5:00 P.M., allow them to play or watch television until precisely 7:15, when she would bathe them so they might be in bed by 8:00.

"On this particular night, since it was very warm outside, the boys chose to sit quietly and watch cartoons on television," Tammy recalled. "They were unusually quiet while I tidied up the kitchen, and I had just been mentally remarking to myself that, generally speaking, Dale and I had been blessed with trouble-free children.

"I was just putting away the last of the dinner dishes when little Curtis staggered into the kitchen with his arms outstretched toward me. His eyes were wide with fear and obvious discomfort, and his mouth was opening and closing, making gasping and sucking sounds, as if he were having trouble breathing properly."

Tammy rushed to Curtis and knelt to take him in her arms. "What is it, honey? Can you tell Mommy what's wrong?"

As she began to lift the child, he suddenly went limp in her arms.

"I kept telling myself not to panic," Tammy said, "but what can frighten a mother more than her baby suddenly losing consciousness with her not knowing the cause?"

She loosened Curtis's clothing, then examined his head for any bumps or bruises.

"When I found no physical marks of any kind, I really started to become frightened," Tammy said. "I didn't know what to do. I called Jimmy into the room and as calmly as possible asked him if he knew what was the matter with his brother. He just stared at me blankly and shook his head in the negative."

Tammy carried Curtis to the sink to wash his face and head with cool water. If that didn't bring him around, she resolved to take no further chances. She would call the doctor immediately.

Tammy was nearly to the sink when she felt a stinging slap on her back. Startled, she turned around to see nothing or no one who could have dealt her such a sharp blow.

"But it was at that point that I distinctly heard a deep masculine voice ordering me to turn Curtis upside down and to place my finger down his throat," she said. "Stunned, confused, wondering if stress was causing me to lose my mind, I stood there immobile, helplessly clutching little Curtis to my chest."

Two more smart slaps stung her shoulder and brought her out of her temporary paralysis.

"Quickly!" the voice demanded. "If you wish to save your son's life, hold his head down and put your finger down his throat!"

Tammy felt weak, dizzy. Could such things really be

happening to her?

Yet another powerful, stinging slap on her shoulder emphasized the urgency of the voice's commands: "Hurry! To save your son's life, you must act now!"

Prodded at last into obedience by the demands of the stern voice and the smart blows on her shoulder, Tammy turned baby Curtis over her knee with his head down and stuck her finger down his throat.

She managed to dislodge a pink lump of the children's clay that she had always feared might smell and taste too good to remain simply something to be molded and not eaten.

Little Curtis sucked in a deep gasp of air and began to cry. Tammy sobbed with relief that the crisis seemed to have passed and that her baby appeared to be all right.

"When Curtis's lusty screams had been reduced to soft whimpers, I once again had the presence of mind to look about the kitchen, seeking some clue to the source of the remarkable experience with the unseen voice that had saved my child's life," Tammy said.

"I asked Jimmy—who had stood in the kitchen open-mouthed in wonder throughout the entire episode— if he had heard a voice talking to me. The commands were so loud and clear I would have suspected that our neighbors in the duplex might have heard them."

Tammy recalled that Jimmy shook his head and

replied, "No, Mommy. There is no one here besides me, and I was too scared to say anything!"

Later that night, as she prepared for bed, Tammy remained baffled by the sound of the mysterious voice and the impact of the stinging blows from an invisible hand.

"I was about to step into the tub for a good, hot bath when I was astonished to see quite clearly a series of reddened, weltlike marks across my shoulders. Hours later I could still distinguish the imprints of what certainly appeared to be human fingers in the flesh of my back."

Tammy fell asleep that night with fervent prayers of thanks on her lips. She knew that the voice had saved her son's life, and she did not mind at all the stinging slaps that had prompted her into action and into obedience.

When Dale returned the next afternoon with his catch of fish, the stories that accompanied each marine trophy paled into insignificance when Tammy told him of the miraculous rescue of their son by an unseen entity.

"Although Dale has never been a particularly religious man," Tammy said, "he told me that he firmly believed that the voice that I had heard belonged to Curtis's guardian angel. Dale said that in his opinion, it simply wasn't our baby's time to return to Heaven, and his angel saw to it that he be granted a longer period of time on Earth to learn and to grow."

On September 11, 1991, Geraldo Silva was standing outside an apartment building in Rio de Janeiro, Brazil, waiting for a friend to join him, when something caused him to look up. Plummeting headfirst toward him was a baby!

Instinctively, Silva knew that the child would surely die if it struck the sidewalk, so he stuck out his arms as if he were about to catch a football. The baby's impact knocked them both to the sidewalk.

Dazed by the sudden and incredible drama in which he found himself an impromptu participant, Silva examined his surprise catch from the sky and believed the little girl was dead. Blood was pouring from her mouth.

He could see now that the baby was small, probably only twenty pounds or so, but when she landed in his arms, she had felt like a 100-pound sack of grain.

"Mama," the child cried in a weak voice warped by fear and pain.

Silva thanked God that the baby that had dropped down on him from somewhere up above was still alive. He called for help, and one of the shaken passersby who had gathered as witnesses to the remarkable event offered to drive them both to a hospital.

Najwa Safatli had been washing dishes in their seventh-floor apartment when she heard the sound of glass breaking in the living room. Startled, she thought immediately of her eighteen-month-old daughter Jasmin, who was seated in a highchair in front of a window. Could little Jasmin have somehow managed to crawl out of the highchair and broken a vase or some other glass object?

When Najwa entered the living room, she was shocked to see that Jasmin was not in her highchair and that the window behind the chair was broken.

The young mother searched the living room, calling for her daughter. She could not yet allow herself to think the unthinkable. Jasmin could not have fallen out of the window. Perhaps a large bird or something had broken the window and frightened her baby. Jasmin must be somewhere in the apartment.

Najwa Safatli told journalist Christina Menzies that when she finally looked out the window, she was horrified to see that a crowd had gathered on the street below. At about the same time, a neighbor pounded on the apartment door and told Najwa that Jasmin had fallen out of the window and had been taken to a hospital.

Najwa was certain that Jasmin, their only child, was dead. She believed that it would be impossible for an eighteen-month-old child—or anyone else, for that matter—to fall out of a seventh-floor window and survive.

Frantic, she didn't wait for the elevator but ran barefooted down the stairs to the parking garage in the apartment building. She rushed to the hospital, trying to calm herself to expect the worst. Once she learned Jasmin's fate, she would call her husband, Ahmad, who was at work.

When the doctors at the hospital told the fearful mother that Jasmin was alive, Najwa said that she knew a miracle had occurred. Her baby had suffered only a broken leg and some bruises. Najwa thanked God and blessed Geraldo Silva for saving Jasmin's life.

Silva shrugged off all attempts to categorize him as a

hero. In his opinion, a benevolent fate had placed him at precisely the spot so that he might be able to catch little Jasmin as she hurtled through the air to the street below.

As the Safatli family re-created the accident, it appeared that Jasmin had stood up on the seat of her highchair and had lost her balance. Although she weighed only twenty-two pounds, she apparently struck the window with enough force to break it and to fall through it. According to a witness, Jasmin had bounced off an awning on the fifth floor, which slowed her descent to some degree.

But it was forty-five-year-old refrigeration technician Geraldo Silva who completed the miracle by being in exactly the right place at the right time to reach out his arms and catch Jasmin before she landed headfirst on the sidewalk.

In November 1992, twenty-two-month-old Joshua Beatty fell nine stories out of an open window of a Southfield, Michigan, apartment and survived unharmed. In a strange kind of baby miracle, little Joshua's diaper snagged on a bush and cushioned his fall.

A maintenance worker, who witnessed the miraculous incident, said that it was as if God had held out his hands and caught the little boy.

Gina Beatty, Joshua's mother, panicked when she entered his bedroom and saw that the screen had been pushed out of the window. When she realized her baby was nowhere in sight, she was shocked out of her wits.

When she first looked out the window in Joshua's room, she saw two girls on a balcony across the courtyard staring downward in horror. Then Gina heard awful shrieks from below. Forcing herself to look down on the concrete below, she felt her heart thumping her chest as she saw Joshua's diaper on a bush. And then she heard him screaming. He was still alive!

Rushing downstairs as quickly as possible, not knowing in what condition she would find her son, she was astonished to find him standing naked, surrounded by a small crowd of incredulous bystanders. As Joshua ran to her arms, Gina collapsed, shaking uncontrollably.

Miraculously, Joshua's diaper had snagged on a bush only feet from the concrete pavement. Then, somehow, the diaper held his weight long enough for him to hang suspended for a few moments before it snapped and allowed him to tumble harmlessly to the ground.

The experience and training that he had received as a wide receiver when he played high school football may have given park worker Don Hughes the steady hands and nerves that enabled him to catch eighteen-month-old Lydell Craig when the baby fell from a third-story window.

On June 6, 1994, thirty-year-old Hughes and three fellow workers from the Baltimore Parks and Recreation Department were mowing around trees and shrubs when he noticed a crowd gathering outside an apartment building across the street. There was a senior citizens' home nearby, and a lot of elderly men and women were shouting and pointing upward.

Hughes looked up and saw a baby sitting on a third-story window ledge. In spite of the crowd milling around beneath him, the baby, little eighteen-month-old Lydell Craig, sat on the ledge, seemingly unaware of danger and happily taking in the new perspective. A woman, obviously the child's mother, was screaming at the baby, calling him by name, and telling him to please get back into the apartment.

Don Hughes had always been a religious person. And he felt that God had used him on a previous occasion in 1992 to rescue seven of his neighbors who had been trapped in a fire in a rooming house. When Hughes saw little Lydell Craig teetering on his perch three stories above the street, he heard God telling him to get over there fast.

He was walking across the street when the crowd

screamed as if in one voice. The baby on the ledge was falling.

Hughes dashed forward and made the catch of his life. The momentum of his fall took Lydell Craig down to within an inch or two of the concrete, but Hughes's powerful arms saw to it that the baby didn't touch it.

Lydell's mother, Shervonne, told journalist James McCandlish that Don Hughes had performed a miracle and that she would forever be grateful to him. She had left Lydell in her uncle's care when she had gone shopping. Apparently when the uncle wasn't looking, the eighteen-month-old baby had crawled to the open window and had crawled out on the ledge to explore new territory. If a fast-acting Don Hughes hadn't heeded the orders he received from God to run across the street in time to catch little Lydell, the infant would likely have crashed to the concrete and died.

Doctors at the hospital in Mississauga, Ontario, pronounced two-year-old Joey Rodden to be the luckiest little boy that they had ever seen.

Early one morning in April 1996, Joey climbed onto a windowsill of the family's third-floor apartment while he was playing with his four-year-old brother, Robbie. The boys started throwing their toys out of a torn screen as a game. As they were tossing toys out the window, Joey lost his balance and plunged thirty-five feet to the pavement below.

Joey's five-year-old sister, Krystal, saw him fall out the window and ran into her parents' bedroom to tell them the awful news. Cherie and Gary Rodden rushed to the window and looked down in horror to see their son's limp little body lying on the pavement below. There had been no bush or any snow to break his fall, and he lay still, facedown.

Cherie admitted later that she was hysterically praying for a miracle when she and her brother Jon, who was staying with the Roddens, rushed down the stairs.

Jon got to Joey first, knelt beside him, and gently rolled him over on his back. Then his mother's heartfelt prayer for a miracle was granted. Joey opened his eyes, hugged his Uncle Jon, and got to his feet on his own.

When the paramedics arrived and gave the boy a preliminary examination, they were astonished to find that Joey bore not a single scratch, bruise, or mark of any kind. To the contrary, rather than severe or fatal injuries, the paramedics found the biggest problem was restraining Joey from wiggling free from their examination and running off to play with his brother.

Doctors insisted that the miracle tot be taken to the

hospital for two nights of observation, but the medical personnel were unable to find anything wrong with the extremely fortunate two-year-old Joey, who had fallen thirty-five feet without sustaining a single injury.

Truly, the Rodden family agreed, God had sent an angel to watch over their little Joey that morning. With grim humor, they joked that Joey was, indeed, a bouncing baby boy.

Two-year-old Derek Anthony Darden of Bakersfield, California, fell out of a second-story window on May 19, 2002, and survived with only a few scratches.

The Darden family was still sleeping on Sunday morning when their neighbor rang the doorbell and informed them that their two-year-old son had fallen out of a window and onto the paved parking lot. It appeared that Derek, who shared a room with a seven-month-old brother, had pushed the crib against the window and had crawled up to check things out. And then ended up falling out.

After examining the two-year-old at a hospital, doctors released him to his parents, pronouncing Derek free from injury, except for a couple of scratches. The miracle baby's father quipped that he guessed drinking milk really did make a tot strong and healthy.

When Jenny was a young mother of twenty-four, she learned that miracles don't necessarily come like a clap of thunder to announce their arrival. Sometimes, she said, they come softly, unassumingly, like a baby's breath.

As Jenny tells the story:

It was 1971, and I learned I was expecting my second child. In and of itself I found this miraculous, due to many medical problems over the past few years. After the birth of my daughter, aged two, I had been unable to carry a pregnancy past eight weeks, and I had been told that to expect another child was doubtful indeed.

My doctor had told me not to get my hopes up, or I would just be all the more disappointed. He seemed quite certain that it was inevitable I would lose the baby that I was carrying. I, on the other hand, never doubted his arrival.

And arrive he did, on a day with a soft Arizona rain falling outside. He was perfect in every way. I named him Andrew William.

Little did I know then what a journey Andy and I would travel together for the next year.

After a few days at home, I went to get Andy from his nap and found him still and lifeless and somewhat blue. He was not breathing.

Thank God, Andy had not died, and I was able to get him to begin breathing again. But as it turned out, this was not the last time I'd experience the panic of a mother who thinks her precious infant's life might have been taken away. I would come into his room again and again to find him lying still, not breathing.

Not much was known at that time of a condition now referred to as Sudden Infant Death Syndrome (SIDS). I am sure we all have heard stories of a mother going into the baby's room and finding, sadly, that the infant had died—suddenly, quietly, with no explanation of what had caused this to occur.

Many doctors' visits and their several opinions left me with no answers as to why my baby seemed constantly to stop breathing. Trips to the hospital for innumerable tests showed no medical reason for this terrible thing to be occurring. For a while, I took every precautionary measure I could think of, including having oxygen tanks and a plastic covering over Andy's crib to help him breathe, yet his breathing problem continued.

I didn't want my baby out of my sight, so I dragged a mattress into his room, and I slept there with Andy night after night. I would prop myself up against the wall with Andy's head on my shoulder, always with his mouth by my ear so that I might listen to the soft sound of his breathing.

Sometimes, I would hear a soft little clicking sound and then he would go limp in my arms. I'd puff in his mouth or shake him a bit, and he seemed to snap out of it. I will admit I did that hard praying that one does when panicked and terrified.

For some reason, Andrew did not seem to be growing as he should, and his baby doctor suggested perhaps his lungs were small or as yet undeveloped.

I refused to consider seriously the growth hormones that the doctors suggested. In my steadfast opinion, Andrew was his own self and did not need drugs, which I felt could cause more harm than good.

I was told that such a point of view was foolishness on my part. The doctors argued that the constant stopping and starting of Andy's breathing could in some way be causing a lack of oxygen to his brain, but once again I refused a growth hormone's being administered to my baby.

Just as stubbornly, the doctors persisted in recommending the hormones. From their perspective, if Andy should receive the drug therapy and begin to grow at a more normal rate, his lungs and other internal organs would grow as well. Even when they administered the growth hormones, they warned me, Andrew would at best reach a height of five feet when fully grown.

My little mother and child story would be as long as Tolstoy's *War and Peace* if I were to account for an entire year of time after time after time seeing my infant son making the frightening transition from being a kicking, smiling, happy baby one moment to a still, blue, lifeless body the next.

One night Andy stopped breathing, and I had tears pouring down my face in fear and frustration.

I puffed in his mouth and he didn't move.

I shook and jiggled him, saying "C'mon, c'mon, breathe, Andrew!"

Once again, nothing.

Sometimes when we are frightened and terrified, we

just throw up our hands in despair and allow other thoughts of shame, defeat, and inadequacy to rush in upon us. I felt that I had paid little attention to my two-year-old daughter during the ordeal with Andy, and I allowed a certain amount of guilt to flood my emotions. My husband worked two jobs at that time, and even though he was working hard to support the family, I suppose I felt quite alone in caring for our son. I also felt as if I had had a total of only five uninterrupted minutes of sleep in the past year. I was beyond tired.

Now I held a limp, blue baby in my arms for what seemed like the millionth time, and all I could think of at that awful moment was to yell at him to knock it off. To this day, I recall just yelling at him, "Andy, this is your mother talking to you. Knock off this business about stopping your breathing right now!"

And poor Andy was getting bluer by the second.

I prayed with all my heart and begged God to touch my child and to restore his health, to make Andrew breathe.

I believe in the power of prayer. I also believe in miracles. I prayed that this thing, this condition, this hardship on an innocent child would stop.

Something far bigger than I was needed in this desperate situation. At this point, I felt overwhelmingly powerless. I prayed that God would allow me to see a miracle enter our lives, as I was lost as to what to do.

Perhaps this is what we call "Giving it all up to God," as I felt at that moment that Andy and I had reached the end of our journey together. There was a time when I believed that if I never put Andy down or out of my sight, maybe I could fix the problem with my eternal vigilance. But at this early-morning hour, I felt my human failure. I knew I couldn't do a thing.

I was not particularly religious, but suddenly God was all that stood between me and losing my little boy. I had faith that there was a higher power that could do all things.

I remembered something from the Bible; and grasping at straws, I said the words out loud: "Suffer the little children to come unto Me."

I wasn't really certain at that time what those words meant, but I was to learn.

As I held Andrew up to my ear, I heard a huge gasp of an intake of air.

Never again did Andy stop breathing.

Today, over thirty years later, this young man is the kindest human being I have ever known in my life. He is beautiful of face. He is beyond what any mother would wish for in a son.

Am I prejudiced? Certainly.

As far as his being short of stature, Andrew is well

over six feet tall. As for any brain damage from this ordeal, he has been blessed with exceptional intelligence. He has a master's degree, and he will soon receive a second master's from the University of Arizona.

Some might read my story and say that it was just the luck of the draw that Andy made it, but I disagree. My experience with my child taught me that miracles can happen. That God hears all prayers. That a miracle isn't always accompanied by a choir of angels or a golden light filling the room to announce that it has arrived.

No, my friends, sometimes miracles come when all faith is seemingly gone and we need one the most.

And sometimes they arrive as quietly as the sound of a baby softly breathing.

*I*n 1992, at the age of two, little Nicole Thomas developed neuroblastoma, one of the most serious types of childhood cancers. Medical experts grimly state that the survival rate is less than 5 percent. Nicole's parents, Mark and Erika, were shocked when they were told that the six-pound tumor inside their little girl was wrapped around every major organ in her body. And they were dismayed when the doctors told them they were unable to operate on Nicole because they were not able to determine where her liver ended and the tumor started.

Although the doctors did not wish to be unfeeling, they decided that they should be frank and tell the Thomases that it would be best if they took Nicole home to die. In their professional medical opinion, it simply was not worth putting the little girl through the pain and discomfort of an extended treatment of chemotherapy. According to their considered diagnoses, Nicole had only three months to live.

Mark and Erika weighed the doctors' pronouncement very seriously. They discussed their options, then prayed to God and asked for guidance in making the right decision.

That evening when Nicole's principal doctor at the Children's Medical Center in the large southwestern city came to check on his patient, Erika and Mark told her that they were planning on a miracle. They wished Nicole to begin chemotherapy treatments.

The Thomases and their three other children, Joseph, David, and Patricia, prayed a lot as little Nicole underwent the pain and suffering of the chemotherapy treatments. Nicole didn't die within the three-month period that the doctors had given her to live, and in spite of the doctors' prior predictions of her imminent death, the tumor within her kept getting smaller and smaller. After six months, the once deadly tumor that had intertwined itself around her major organs was nearly gone.

At that point, the doctors operated on Nicole and removed the remainder of the growth.

Praising God for granting them the miracle of shrinking the tumor to the size where it could be safely excised from Nicole's little body, the Thomases were once again saddened when the doctors informed them that the cancer was now attacking her bone marrow.

Accepting the challenge of the new fight, the Thomases continued to pray for another miracle for their baby and gave the doctors permission to use a new medical treatment on the cancer. The skillful doctors at the Children's Medical Center removed Nicole's bone marrow and treated it with special antibodies while, at the same time, giving the little girl radiation and chemotherapy treatments.

This time the renewed campaign of advanced medical science and the power of prayer triumphed over the vicious enemy of cancer. Nicole was granted another miracle.

Today, Nicole is a healthy twelve-year-old whose memories of having had cancer and having undergone a great deal of pain grow dimmer with each passing year. She appreciates the blessing of having been given another chance, and she hopes one day to enter some aspect of the medical field and be able to help alleviate the pain of others.

When nine-year-old Scotty Baston of Grapevine, Texas, received the 1996 White Helmet Award for heroism for his bravery in saving two-year-old Sean Maloney from drowning, all those in attendance at the award ceremony agreed with Scotty's mother, Joanne, that her son had accomplished a miracle. Scotty suffers from Angelman syndrome, which rendered him mentally retarded and unable to speak.

Although Scotty may not have realized that he saved a life, Joanne Baston told reporter Ruth Watts, he knew that he had done something good because everyone was making such a fuss over him. Physically nine years old, Scotty had about the same mental development as a three-year-old.

On that particular afternoon, neighborhood children had gathered to play in the Baston's swimming pool. When Danielle Maloney, Sean's mother, began to gather her kids, she removed the two-year-old's water wings preparatory to leaving. However, the moment that she turned her back to see to her other children, little Sean jumped unnoticed back into the pool. He immediately slipped below the surface of the water and was soon in great danger of drowning.

Unable to speak or call out for help from the adults whose attention was momentarily distracted from the pool, Scotty watched as the two-year-old boy struggled in the water.

Victims of Angelman syndrome, a disease that affects 1 in 25,000 people, are very often affectionate and happy individuals, but, sadly, are handicapped by severe mental retardation, inability to speak, and unstable, jerky body movements. But as Scotty's mother said, a miracle occurred. Somehow he sensed that little Sean was in trouble, and he reached down and lifted the boy out of the water.

Fire Chief Bill Powers, who made the decision to

give Scotty the award for heroism, said that Scotty had been alert enough to know that the two-year-old was in great difficulty and reacted as a true hero by removing Sean immediately from the swimming pool.

Joanne Baston was proud of her son and said that Scotty's actions demonstrated that even those children who are severely handicapped may still have wonderful gifts to share with others. People should never put limits on what such individuals might be able to do, she commented.

*I*magine what it would be
like being born a twin —
but having to celebrate
your birthdays ninety-five days apart. That's exactly the
case with twins Timothy and Celeste Keys, who were
born a record-setting three months apart.

On October 15, 1994, Timothy entered the world
three months prematurely. The doctors and nurses
waited and waited for Celeste to join her twin brother,
but she stubbornly refused to budge.

Dr. Jay Goldsmith of the Oschner Foundation
Hospital in New Orleans had been advised that Simone

Keys was going to deliver two very small, premature babies, but no one had been able to predict the unusual circumstances that he and the medical staff faced when one of the twins remained fast in the womb. However, since the mother's contractions had ceased, the doctors decided to attempt to seize the opportunity to allow Celeste to remain in her mother's womb to give her more time to develop.

The doctors and nurses tipped Simone upside down and sewed her cervix shut, thereby keeping her sac from breaking. They then directed all attention toward saving Timothy's life. He had weighed in at just one pound, fourteen ounces.

Timothy was immediately placed in a ventilator in the neonatal unit of the hospital, and he was closely monitored while he gained strength and weight. Unfortunately, it was determined that he had suffered a brain hemorrhage that could cause eye problems and learning disabilities, but the doctors were optimistic that he would outgrow such potential difficulties.

Celeste was born three months later without any complications, thereby making Rev. Thomas and Simone Keys of New Orleans the parents of a record-breaking set of twins. The separated pair broke the previous record of fifty-six days that had been established in 1956 by a woman with a double uterus.

By the time that his sister was born in January 1995, Timothy had gained enough weight to tip the scales at five pounds, two ounces, while Celeste weighed about six pounds at birth.

In addition to the twins, Simone Keys, a high school English teacher, and her husband Thomas, pastor of the Bright Morning Star Baptist Church in New Orleans, also had a three-year-old son, Thomas Jr. Pastor Keys stated that their having added the miracle twins to their family had made the world seem like heaven.

*T*hirty-five-year-old Suzanne Falkenhagen of rural Alabama told us that when her youngest daughter, Margaret, was nine months old, she and her husband feared they would lose her.

"That was back in September of 1988," Suzanne told us. "Little Margaret had cried most of her tiny life, and to quiet her I had to carry her in my arms practically all day long. She was very thin and had grown but little."

One evening Suzanne's husband, Paul, decided to sleep with their two-year-old son, Richard, in the other bedroom.

"Paul was doing heavy manual labor at that time, and he needed to get his rest," Suzanne explained. "We had only been married a little over three years, and we had been having some pretty tough times. We hadn't been able to continue to make rent for the nice house that we had been living in before the kids came, and we were just making ends meet in a pretty ramshackle house that needed a lot of repairs. We couldn't afford to have Paul miss any work time, and it was nearly impossible for him to get any sleep at all in our bedroom with poor little Margaret crying most of the night."

At last the baby fell asleep, and Suzanne eased the child down on the bed beside her.

"I was too much on edge to nod off right away, so I picked up the Bible from the nightstand and opened the pages at random to Matthew 11. Soon I was reading verses twenty-eight to thirty, which invite all to come to Jesus for their restoration: 'Come unto me, all ye that labor and are heavy laden, and I will give you rest. Take my yoke upon you, and learn of me; for I am meek and lowly in heart: and ye shall find rest unto your souls. For my yoke is easy, and my burden is light.'"

Suzanne felt as though the verses had been written directly to her.

"I sat up in bed and thought for a minute," Suzanne said. "Although I was definitely weary and 'heavy

laden'—and I certainly needed some rest—I realized
with shame that even though I professed to be a good
Christian, I had not read my Bible nor had I prayed very
much at all since the baby was born.

"I knew that my recent motherhood should be no
excuse, but I had so much trouble with Margaret that it
seemed that every waking moment was spent with her.
We had taken her to the doctor several times, and he had
given her medications. But Margaret cried practically all
day and night."

Suzanne slowly moved away from the baby and
buried her face in her pillow. "I prayed to Jesus to give
me some sign that his love was forever and that he was
still there to bless me. I thanked him that he had given
Margaret life, and I begged him to heal her. Then I
asked forgiveness for having neglected my Bible reading
and my daily prayers."

Suzanne looked up and was startled to behold Jesus
sitting on the end of a trunk beside the bed.

"He was dressed in a long, dark robe tied with a
fairly thick white cord. His brownish hair was shoulder-
length, and his brown eyes were warm and filled with
love. I also noticed that he wore leather sandals."

Suzanne said that Jesus was "the most soft spoken,
loving person" that she had ever met. "I could feel
waves of warmth and love moving around me as he

quoted several scripture passages to me to prove that I was a member of his flock and because of his great sacrificial act of redemption."

Suzanne told Jesus of her great love for him and for God and for all those who tried to follow a good and moral life. "He talked to me for at least ten or twelve minutes, and he convinced me that he loved me and would always be with me," she said. "Then he stood up and walked to the center of the bedroom, just below the ceiling that was being repaired.

"He turned and looked back at me and told me not to worry anymore about the baby and about our future. He said that things would steadily get better for us. 'I will be with you and your family forever,' he said."

Suzanne told us that after Jesus had spoken those words, he rose, and she "watched him pass through the shingles as if he were a cloud of smoke."

Within two or three days after the visitation by Jesus, she said, her baby was completely well and little Margaret had ceased her seemingly endless cries of discomfort.

"All of our family was happy," she concluded. "And whenever any of us ever became glum, I reminded them of the glorious visitation by Jesus and his wonderful words that he would be with us forever."

Twenty-nine-year-old Cheryl Gardner told us that she was certain that she would have died when she collapsed from insulin shock if her two-year-old son, Robbie, hadn't been there to punch in the 911 call.

"I have been diabetic since I was in my late teens, so I should have been more aware that my blood sugar was getting low," Cheryl said. "It was on April 3, 1999, and I had gotten off work early so that I could get our house in order for my husband's surprise birthday party that night. I had skimped on breakfast and skipped lunch completely so I could work through the break and not upset my boss when I left at three instead of five o'clock."

Her six-year-old daughter, Norma, was helping by washing dishes in the kitchen, and little Robbie was with Cheryl in the recreation room when she began to feel the initial symptoms that should have warned her to take a break and get a snack to boost her blood sugar.

"I was elaborately decorating the room with streamers and posters, hoping to make Adam's breaking the Big 3-0 a little less painful, when my hands started shaking," she said. "Unfortunately, I was just too preoccupied with decorating the room to notice the first symptoms of hypoglycemia or insulin shock."

Cheryl continued working, ignoring the fact that she was sweating profusely. After all, she was climbing a ladder, stretching and bending, placing colorful signs and posters all around the recreation room. And it was hot that day in the suburb of Dallas, Texas, where they lived.

And then the dizziness hit her. With blurred vision, her arms and legs shaking violently, Cheryl managed to get down from the ladder and crawl to the sofa that she had pushed against a wall.

At first, little Robbie thought his mother was playing with him, crawling on all fours like a big doggie or a monster that would grab him and tickle him.

"Thinking he was beating me at the tickle game, Robbie came to the sofa, laughing and digging his little fingers into my ribs to make me laugh," Cheryl said. "I remember having a splitting headache, and then all around me everything went black. As I was slipping into a coma, I hoped that I was still able to whisper, '911 . . . call 911.'"

Later, when she regained consciousness, Cheryl remembered the taste of sugar on her lips. A fire-rescue team was there at her side, along with Robbie and Norma.

"We had preset dialing for 911," Cheryl said, "and Robbie had punched it in as soon as I had entered the coma due to insulin shock. Then he had run to get his six-year-old sister, who, very much aware of my condition, got some sugar cubes and forced them into my mouth. Although the sugar wasn't enough to revive me, it certainly helped prevent me from entering an even deeper comatose state."

After the paramedics had given Cheryl an injection of insulin and some oxygen, she had a snack of a peanut butter sandwich and a can of soda. Although she was a bit shaky, she was still able to be a charming hostess at her husband's thirtieth birthday party that night.

"Thank God, we had demonstrated the preset 911 button for Robbie, and he had the presence of mind to punch it just as soon as I slipped into a comatose state," she said. "Norma had finished her chores and had gone into the living room to watch cartoons on television. It might have been a half hour or more before she came to the rec room to check on things. If it hadn't been for Robbie's quick action, the insulin shock that I suffered might have become life-threatening."

An astonishing report in the November 14, 2002, issue of the Norwegian newspaper *Aftenposten* told of a woman who regained her sight through the miracle of childbirth.

Twenty-nine-year-old Mona Ramdal was born with toxoplasmosis, an infection that can cause eye or brain damage in infants. Because of the infection, Mona's right eye has always been afflicted with limited vision; and when she turned thirteen, her left eye also began to fail. Eventually, Mona had only 15 percent vision remaining in her left eye and scarcely any in her right eye.

But when she became pregnant, a most wonderful series of miracles appeared to be set in motion. The sight in Mona's left eye began to return. By the time her daughter Anne-Marthe was born in 2001, Mona could see. Within a few months after Anne-Marthe's birth, Mona applied for a driver's license and passed the tests on her first attempt.

Dr. Per Hvamstad, who has treated Mona Ramdal since the late 1970s when she was a little girl, said that he had never read or heard of a similar case of loss of eyesight restored through pregnancy. Since the retina is by medical definition a part of the brain, Dr. Hvamstad explained, once it is destroyed, it is gone forever. That is why, in his opinion, the restoration of vision in someone such as Mona Ramdal, who was terribly visually impaired, must be considered a miracle.

ane Keller told us that in the early summer months of 1997, their nine-year-old son, Todd, had been awakened by the same awful nightmare every night for several weeks. In each of the terrible dreams, he saw his little two-year-old sister, Jennifer, fall into a deep, dark lake and drown.

"There were no large bodies of water around us in the section of New Jersey in which we lived," Jane said, "so my husband, Paul, and I did our best to soothe Todd and convince him that Baby Jenny wasn't going to drown in any lake.

"We then convinced ourselves that we had been permitting him to watch too many television shows with violent content. We agreed to monitor more closely Todd's television viewing and to be more aware of what images he could be seeing that might translate into dreams of his sister drowning."

The Kellers assured themselves that Todd's nightmares did not disguise any feelings of resentment or hostility toward his baby sister. While some of their well-intentioned relatives had warned the couple that they shouldn't have waited so long before having a second child and that Todd had been their one and only for so long that he was liable to feel jealous of the new baby, Todd had prided himself on being Jennifer's big brother even before she was born. Then, from the moment that she had been brought home and placed in a crib in the nursery, Todd had demonstrated nothing but loving care toward his little sister.

"Because we were so convinced that Todd's nightmares were not to be taken seriously, we thought nothing of planning our summer vacation at a lake resort in Maine," Jane said. "It simply never occurred to either Paul or myself that Todd might be having what is known as a precognitive dream of an actual future occurrence. Neither of us had ever been into ESP, the supernatural, or the mystical. And I'm afraid neither of us had ever even been considered very religious. So I am afraid that we could not imagine the horror that must have gripped Todd's heart when we announced Moose Lake in Maine as our vacation spot."

Jane recalled that Todd had almost begun to cry when they told him where they were going. "He pleaded with us to go some other place," Jane said. "He began to list a number of locations that were far inland and had nothing to do with large bodies of water."

One night at dinner, Paul became impatient, and he gruffly told his son that if he didn't want to travel with them to Moose Lake, perhaps he would rather stay home in New Jersey with his grandparents.

Without hesitation, Todd had readily agreed. "But Jennifer has to stay with me at Grandma and Grandpa Keller's," he added. "Jennifer can't go to Moose Lake. She can't go where there's a lot of water."

Jennifer looked up from her peas from her seat in the highchair and frowned in protest over what she thought she had heard. "I want to go wif Mommy and Daddy."

Jane reached over to pat Jennifer's arm and assure her that everyone was going to go together wherever they went.

Paul frowned and quietly set down his knife and fork. "It's that dream again, isn't it?" he asked Todd.

"You've been having those nightmares about Jenny drowning again."

Todd avoided his father's eyes and seemed suddenly very interested in his mashed potatoes. "I haven't been having them every night, like I was," he finally admitted. "But when I have them, I remember them. I don't want anything to happen to Jenny."

And then, Jane remembered, Todd did begin to cry, and he asked to be excused from the table.

After Todd had left the dining room, Paul and Jane discussed whether or not they should change their plans and make arrangements to travel somewhere other than Moose Lake for their vacation. They didn't want to spoil Todd's vacation—or theirs—because of his obsession with a bad dream.

"We decided, however, that even nine-year-old boys have to face their fears," Jane said. "Paul said that we would never do anything cruel, such as forcing Todd to enter the lake if he didn't wish to, but perhaps if at first we just went boating or fishing or some other activity that was fun to do on the water, we might eventually all go swimming and slowly, gently, allow Todd to see that his bad dreams weren't destined to come true."

As soon as they arrived at the resort and had checked into their cabin, Paul suggested that they all go for a boat ride. It was a bright sunny day, and while Jane saw to it that the kids had plenty of sunblock to prevent severe burning, Paul made the arrangements to rent a boat for the afternoon.

"From time to time, Todd would reach over and check the ties on Jenny's bright orange life vest," Jane said. "Although visibly nervous about being on the water, Todd eventually got into the spirit of skimming across the lake's surface in a powerful motorboat. He even laughed when, on occasion, water would spray over us."

After an afternoon of boating and a hearty meal of fresh fish early that evening, both Todd and Jenny fell into a deep sleep in their bunk beds in the cabin. Paul and Jane were relieved when it seemed as though Todd would be able to sleep through the night without suffering another of his terrible nightmares.

When Todd awakened early the next morning, he was startled to see that Jenny was not in the bunk below him. He crawled down the wooden ladder and walked barefooted across the room to look in on his parents in their bedroom. When he saw that they were still asleep and that Jenny had not snuggled in between them, Todd knew with a complete and total certainty that she had gone to the lake by herself.

If Todd had not been seized by the awful memories

of his nightmares and had not been thrown into a state of panic, he would have known that he should have awakened his sleeping parents. But all the nine-year-old could think about was his little sister's falling into the lake and drowning.

"As we later understood the sequence of events," Jane explained, "Todd ran from the cabin to the dock several yards away where he spotted Jenny standing on the end, facing the lake. She had wrapped a piece of string around a stick and was 'fishing' off the end of the dock. Still barefooted, Todd began to tip-toe on the dock toward his two-year-old sister. He knew better than to shout at her, for that might frighten her and she could lose her balance."

In spite of these cautions, Jenny suddenly leaned forward to inspect more closely the string that she dangled in the water to catch a fish and fell into the lake.

"When Todd saw Jenny fall into the lake, he totally freaked out," Jane said. "By the time that he got to the end of the dock, Jenny was in the water, splashing, gasping for air, her little head bobbing first below, then above, the surface of the lake. There was no one else nearby who could help, so Todd knew that it was up to him to save his sister's life. There was no way that he would permit the horrifying nightmares of Jenny's death by drowning to occur in real life, so he jumped in the lake and swam as fast as he could to Jenny, who was already sinking."

Todd told his parents later that he went under, grabbed Jenny around the waist, and lifted her head out of the water. Then he tried to get to shore.

But the two-year-old panicked. And as Jenny struggled in fear, she began to force Todd's head under the water. Todd knew that he was in trouble. He couldn't hold his breath any longer, so he came up and screamed for help.

"That was when my mother's ESP kicked into action," Jane said. "At that very moment, I was having a dream that my children were in danger. I don't remember exactly what was threatening them, but somehow I heard Todd's scream in my very heart and soul. I sat bolt upright in bed and yelled for Paul to wake up. I grabbed my bathrobe, quickly wrapped it around me, and ran out of the cabin."

Intuitively, Jane headed for the dock, and she screamed for help when she saw Todd valiantly attempting to keep both his sister and himself afloat. Both Jane and Paul were excellent swimmers, and they were able to retrieve their children from the lake within a matter of moments.

"Neither Todd nor Jenny was the worse for wear after the rescue," Jane said. "Todd said that all that mattered was that his beloved little sister was all right.

"Later, after some warm cocoa and toast, Todd told us that he knew that his worries—and his nightmares— were now over," Jane said, concluding her account. "What he had seen in his terrible dreams had now occurred in real life. Jenny had fallen into the water, just as he had seen in his nightmares. But she didn't drown. We had been able to rescue her. Todd said that now he would always know that the love of our family could conquer any bad thing that might try to hurt any one of us."

Our friend Barbara May shared a beautiful story of the healing of her infant daughter's viral pneumonia through the grace of Mother Mary.

"It was in January 1960 that my four-month-old daughter, Laura, was admitted to the City of Hope Hospital in Duarte, California," Barbara said. "At that time it seemed as though most admissions were done with the understanding that there was little hope of the patient's recovering. Laura was admitted with viral pneumonia in both lungs, and we were given little promise that she could be saved."

The infant was placed on the critical list for six days with private nurses in attendance around the clock.

On the afternoon of the sixth day, Barbara felt that she needed a break from the stress of being at her daughter's bedside and went to see the woman who was at that time her mother-in-law.

"She suggested that we walk to her local parish church in Sierra Madre to pray," Barbara recalled. "She remained at the back in one of the pews, and I went up to the front, to the Our Lady side of the church. I lit a candle and began to pray."

Laura is Barbara's second daughter, and she could not bear to accept the reality of her dying.

"I was asking for grace and understanding," she said. "I remember looking up at the statue of Our Lady and thinking that it must be because of my lack of sleep that the statue appeared to be expanding and glowing."

At the same time, Barbara remembered, the church was suddenly filled with an almost overwhelming scent of roses that became so powerful that it was nearly sickening. "I thought at first that only I noticed the scent, but as I walked toward the back of the church, my mother-in-law asked me where the roses were, and she began looking around to see where they might be."

Barbara told us that she can still recall the hush of

the church, the afternoon light falling right where they stood, and the strong, enveloping scent of roses.

"My mother-in-law told me that St. Teresa of Lisieux had the identical experience with the scent of roses when she prayed to the Virgin Mary," Barbara said.

"I did not see the Virgin, but the smell of roses stayed with me until the next morning, when the hospital called and told me that a miracle had occurred: Laura's fever had broken, and she no longer had any trace of a virus or any pneumonia."

When Barbara returned to the hospital that she had left only ten hours before, she found a rosy-cheeked, healthy baby "whose light brown baby fuzz had turned completely white during the night."

Barbara was so excited that Laura was going to live that it was some time before her mother-in-law reminded her of what had happened that day in church.

"It gave me goose bumps then, and it still does, because I believe that the Virgin Mary answered my prayers that day. I know what I experienced, and I had a witness in my mother-in-law. Most of all, in Laura's miraculous recovery I have a result that is undeniable and documented."

*J*anice Gray Kolb told us
that as a little girl she had
almost died from a terrible
episode of pneumonia.

"My case of pneumonia was so serious that Dr.
Fisher, the pediatrician, stayed overnight in our home for
three successive nights," Janice said. "As I was growing
up, I was always grateful to that kind doctor; and when I
became a mother myself, I began taking my little ones to
the same doctor. It was truly unusual to learn my husband had also had this same man as his pediatrician, too."

While it is quite certain that Janice's parents believed

her recovery from the serious case of pneumonia was a miracle, she told us about another miracle that occurred with one of her own babies in August 1963 when Janice and her husband, Bob, decided to take their four children to the shores of the Atlantic at Ocean City, New Jersey, on a weekend mini-vacation.

As Janice relates the story in her own words:

Though my husband and I did not know each other when we were children, this was the place where our families had vacationed when we were growing up. This vacation spot was seventy miles east of our home in a suburb of Philadelphia.

Arriving on a Friday evening, we began our first day there Saturday morning by going out to breakfast on the boardwalk by the sea. Our three daughters, June, Laurel, and Barbara, were then eight, six, and four years old. Our youngest, a son, George, was eighteen months. Though he was the smallest, George ate a hearty breakfast and cleaned his plate. The girls were not big eaters, and while they were finishing their breakfasts, little George was also busy snitching goodies from their plates to complement what he had already eaten. Though we did not realize it then, apparently he had consumed too much.

Pushing George in his stroller, we walked back down the boardwalk to the motel where we had rented two adjoining rooms on the beach. Excited about spending the day jumping waves, building sand castles, and digging on the beach, we began immediately to change into our bathing suits.

Bob and I had just changed our clothing when our daughters called to us from the other room. George had thrown up, then aspirated his vomit back into his trachea before he fell over and became unconscious.

Although we tried to clear his mouth and throat with our fingers and turned him upside down and tried shaking and compression, there was no reviving him. Inwardly panicking, though trying to remain calm, we reached for the telephone. There was no childhood doctor to call there in Ocean City. We did not have a telephone number for the likes of beloved Dr. Fisher, who had saved my life as a little one when I was just George's age. Dr. Fisher had passed away several years before, and the wonderful doctor who had replaced him and presently cared for our children was miles away in Philadelphia.

Bob called the Somers Point Memorial Hospital, telling them the situation. He was told to get to the hospital immediately, and an emergency team would be waiting.

I do not remember details of our piling into our station wagon. I only remember holding my unconscious toddler in my arms, watching for signs of his extremely faint breaths and praying to God with all my heart that he would not stop breathing.

Bob had tied a white handkerchief to the car's aerial. With horn blowing, we sped as fast as we could to the hospital.

Making any kind of time driving was difficult in summer traffic at a shore resort. I personally died a thousand deaths. I kept peering down into George's small face and his almost breathless body, willing him to breathe and wetting him with my tears.

As we continued, we realized that we would soon approach the drawbridge over the bay that connected Ocean City to Somers Point. It was only then, and with great impact, that we realized that if the bridge was up we would lose our son.

In our emergency and frightened state of mind, we had not thought to call the police or any authority so they could arrange for the bridge not to be raised until after we had passed. With a sickening sensation in our stomachs, we remembered that the bridge was frequently raised for large boats. And when it was raised, cars were forced to line up and sometimes had to wait for any amount of time for the bridge to come down, depending on how many boats were passing beneath.

On this day and in those moments our prayers so filled with fervor and cries for help were answered, for when we approached the bridge it was down — and we passed over it as rapidly as traffic and a blaring horn would allow.

When we arrived at the hospital an entire emergency team was waiting in the parking lot to save George. After taking him from my arms and placing him on a gurney, they immediately put an aspirating tube down his throat to clear his trachea. They had an aspirating machine sucking out the tracheal vomitus before we even entered the doors of the emergency room.

And then they whisked him away inside the hospital, and we were directed to a waiting room. In what seemed an eternity, we waited and waited to catch a glimpse of anyone who would give us word of George.

At last a doctor came to inform us that George had survived and would recover. He had, however, developed pneumonia and would be in the hospital at least a week. All that mattered to us was his survival and total recovery. We were so grateful to this medical team that saved his life. Such tears of joy!

The real world began to settle in after this life-giving news. As we continued to wait to be able to see George and go with him to his room, the hard truth suddenly hit me that I had been sitting all this time in a waiting room filled with strangers while wearing only a bathing suit. Though it was a modest one-piece black suit, it is not my nature to walk around like that. Even to the beach I would wear a blouse or covering until we were seated. Now I was surrounded by fully dressed people while barefoot and in a bathing suit!

But my embarrassment soon passed in light of the miracle we had been given, and my attire meant absolutely nothing to me then, knowing that I would soon be holding George in my arms again.

We have always remembered this awful experience when we nearly lost George, and we have thanked God over and over for his mercy in restoring our son to us. To this day I tighten inside just thinking about it.

After Bob and I spent all the visiting hours with George throughout the weekend, Bob had to return to work that Monday. Our two oldest daughters, June and Laurel, stayed in Ocean City with me all week in the motel, and Bob rented a car and took our youngest daughter, Barbara, home to stay with my parents. I would visit George during the two times each day when they would permit me to come. Our girls were too young to be allowed to visit, so they would stand on the grass beneath his window and call up to him. I would hold George at the window so he could wave at his sisters.

Each evening after closing his dental office in Philadelphia, Bob would drive the long distance to Ocean City to meet June, Laurel, and me for dinner. We all have fond memories of meeting at the Somers Point Diner each evening, and we were overjoyed at the recovery George was making. With a favorite stuffed animal in each arm, he became stronger day by day.

Forever, too, we will remember the song that was so popular that summer of 1963. The song makes us smile still, though causing bittersweet memories, for it was "Hello Mudder, Hello Fadder, Here I am in Camp Granada." And in fun and imagination it was as if little George was singing it to us, his "Camp Granada" being the Somers Point Hospital.

After dinner we would all go to that hospital, and Bob and I would spend the visiting hour with George. Bob would then turn around and drive back to Jenkintown, Pennsylvania.

Our son grew to be a wonderful human being who has loved God since he was a small child and who is active in mentoring young people in his church. He has always been involved in sports, and he now serves as the athletic director for a university in Rhode Island. George is married to his lovely wife, Valerie, and they have a four-year-old son and two-year-old twin girls. We are ever grateful to God, who granted George the miracle of survival and a fine life to follow.

It is interesting to note that George's three older sisters (eventually there were two more sisters), who witnessed their little brother's nearly choking to death, all became involved in professional health care. It became a turning point in the life of Barbara, the youngest of the three, and she aspired to be a nurse at a very young age following this event. A favorite playtime was taking care of her dollies in a little nurse's uniform that she received, and she is still a nurse today.

We saw no angels that August morning of 1963, but we know we were surrounded by a band of them as they escorted us quickly to the hospital without incident. Very especially was their presence made known to us in the fact that the drawbridge was down and open to traffic. For had the bridge been up, we know through the authority of George's doctors that I would not be writing this story today.

—JANICE GRAY KOLB,
AUTHOR OF *BENEATH THE STARS AND TREES*

*I*n May 1970, Christine and her husband were elated by the news that they were to become parents. But in November, the couple from Chichester, England, were presented with the doctor's startling diagnosis that the baby had ceased growing.

Christine was devastated by the announcement, assuming at first that the fetus had died at sixth months. But the doctor assured her that there was a discernible heartbeat. It just seemed as though the little girl had stopped growing.

Every week Christine went back for tests, and after

each session she was informed that for some strange reason, Baby Tina's status remained static. She was the same size as the week before.

The original due date for Tina's delivery was February 2, 1971, but that momentous day came and went. Tina seemed in absolutely no hurry to enter the world. And she remained the same size as she had been at the sixth month of the pregnancy.

Dutifully, Christine continued to arrive punctually for her weekly appointment to monitor her baby's development.

Finally, weeks after the original date for Tina's emergence into life beyond the womb, Christine was told that the baby had begun to grow again.

At last, on May 22, 1971, Tina was born, weighing in at a very respectable seven and one-half pounds. Christine had been pregnant for thirteen months; 101 days longer than the norm. *The Guinness Book of Records* verified that her unique term of gestation was the world's longest pregnancy on record.

As Tina was growing up, her mother said that the little girl who had slept so long in her womb would fall asleep while she was being held, bathed, or sitting idly for more than a few moments. Christine could never leave Tina alone when she was giving her a bath for fear she would fall asleep and slip under the water.

When Tina was interviewed in 1994 by journalist Fleur Brennan, the twenty-three-year-old mother of twin girls, Abigail and Laura, said that she could easily sleep twelve hours a night if she forgot to set the alarm. She almost always dozed off whenever the family sat down to watch television.

Dr. Christopher Ruoss, an obstetrician at Worthing and Southlands Hospital in Chichester, commented that it was possible that Tina Houghton slept so much because of the extraordinary time that she had spent in the womb. One could not rule out such a connection, he noted, because Tina is certainly one of a kind.

When the roof of the community center in Bardufoss, Norway, collapsed under the weight of heavy snows on March 11, 2000, Hilde Kristin Stensen became frantic. Her thirteen-month-old daughter, Sunniva, had been playing in the room where the roof and outer walls had caved in.

Hilde Kristin had been in the community center's kitchen when the disaster occurred. She and Sunniva had traveled to the town about 750 miles north of Oslo to be with her soldier husband as he participated in the Joint Winter 2000 exercise that was being conducted by twelve nations. The Norwegian troops were using the community center in Bardufoss as their headquarters during the exercise, and military personnel from the United States, Britain, Germany, and other European nations had their own headquarters elsewhere. All had been peaceful and normal—until without warning the roof and walls had collapsed on the soldiers and their families.

Hilde Kristin rushed to the room where she had last seen Sunniva playing and panicked further when she could not budge the door. She called Sunniva's name, but she could not hear a sound from her to indicate that she was alive. But there were groans and moans from inside the room, telling Hilde Kristin that many people were injured. Perhaps others had been killed by the crush of the snow and the debris of roof and ceiling.

The distraught mother told a Norwegian journalist that she was certain that her baby was dead. Somehow she had to find her husband in all the confusion and destruction, and together they would search for the body of Sunniva under all the snow and rubble.

Just when she was about to be swallowed up by despair and grief, Hilde Kristin heard familiar cries. She turned to see Sunniva in the arms of Second Lieutenant Niels Edie. Her baby was alive, and although very shaken up, seemingly not a great deal worse for the terrible ordeal.

Edie told Hilde Kristin that he had been in the same room with little Sunniva when the roof and walls collapsed. He had seen the baby suddenly covered with snow and rubble; and as soon as he could get to his feet, he had begun digging to free her from beneath the pile of hard-packed snow and debris.

Hilde Kristin praised Edie for his quick action and declared him the Stensen family hero and angel of the day.

Tragically, while a fast-acting, quick-thinking officer had saved a thirteen-month-old baby girl from death that day, three soldiers were killed and ten others injured by the unexpected collapse of the community center's roof.

When Leah was born in 1985, her mother could not help thinking that her baby looked like a little alien visitor from Mars. At six pounds, four ounces, most of Leah's weight was in her head—which was nearly nineteen inches around, just a fraction more than her total body length.

To make matters even worse, the attending physicians' initial diagnosis of Leah was that she was blind, deaf, and born with only a brain stem rather than a complete brain. The little girl would be unable to live for more than a few weeks or months.

A sympathetic nurse told the parents, Tim and Sandy Church, to insist that the doctors drain the fluid from Leah's skull. The doctors knew that the little girl was also afflicted with hydrocephalus, a condition in which the cerebrospinal fluid, instead of circulating around the brain, becomes dammed up inside the cranium and leaves no space for the brain to develop normally. Hydrocephalus is commonly known as "water on the brain," and the doctors told the Churches that draining the fluid from Leah's cranium would not help their daughter in any way. Without wishing to appear cruel or indifferent to their anguish, the doctors once again explained to the Churches that only the brain stem had been allowed to develop in Leah's cranium because of the enormous buildup of fluid.

Sandy pleaded that while the procedure might be pointless from the medical perspective, perhaps it might at least ease little Leah's suffering.

The doctors yielded on the basis of compassion and were astonished to discover that Leah did have more than just a brain stem. The pressure from the buildup of spinal fluid in her skull had so compressed her brain that most of it had not shown up on the previous CAT scan.

Prior to the advent of computerized axial tomography (CAT scans) which facilitates treatment, a physician's prognosis for the 1 in 500 children born with hydrocephalus was quite bleak. Generally doctors predicted a brief life-span, plagued by numerous complications, and little hope of the child's developing normally in either intellectual or physical capacities. With the increased reliance upon the CAT scan and advances in diagnostic imaging technology, most parents may expect the likelihood of normal longevity with little or no intellectual or physical deficiencies.

For four months, the Churches returned to the hospital in Billings, Montana, to have Leah's head drained with a syringe. Eventually, her doctors installed a valve under her scalp so that her parents might pump out the buildup of fluid.

By the age of five, Leah knew the alphabet and could write her name, so the Churches enrolled her in school. Although their daughter had been left with poor eyesight, she was able to progress throughout school with relatively few problems. She even competed in a track meet—a miracle for a child who was said to have been born without a brain.

As dramatic as Leah's case may be, there have been instances in which people have lived with only cerebrospinal fluid and not much more than a brain stem in their craniums—and some of them have done very well. Dr. John Lorber, a neurology professor at the University

of Sheffield in the United Kingdom, acquired a remarkable set of data regarding people who seemed to get
along just fine without complete brains.

In the 1970s when the campus doctor asked Dr.
Lorber to examine a student whose head seemed a bit
larger than normal, Dr. Lorber gave the student a CAT
scan and found that he had virtually no brain at all.
Instead of the normal 4.5-centimeter thickness of brain
tissue between the ventricles and the cortical surface, Dr.
Lorber discovered that the student had only a thin layer
of mantle measuring about a millimeter and that his cranium was filled mainly with cerebrospinal fluid.

The young man had hydrocephalus, a condition that
is often fatal within the first few months of life. In the
1970s, prevailing medical knowledge had it that if individuals with hydrocephalus should survive beyond
infancy, they would usually be severely retarded. However, in the case of the math major from the University of Sheffield, he had an IQ of 126 and graduated
with honors.

Nor was this student as rare as one would imagine.
Dr. Lorber collected research data concerning several
hundred people who functioned quite well with practically no brain at all. Upon careful examination, he
described some of the subjects as having no "detectable
brains." Conventional medicine would state that such

individuals would be completely unable to function on any mental level at all, yet many scored up to 120 in IQ tests. Dr. Lorber theorized that there may be such a high level of redundancy in normal brain function that even the minute particles of brain matter that these people "without brains" did possess might be able to assume the essential activities of a normal-sized brain. Dr. David Bower, professor of neurophysiology at Liverpool University, England, stated that although Dr. Lorber's research does not indicate that the brain is unnecessary, it does demonstrate that amazingly, the brain can work in conditions that conventional medical science usually decrees impossible.

During the early summer of 2000, about four months into her pregnancy, Erin Schuck of Pendleton, Oregon, learned that her baby had a congenital heart condition. According to the doctors, the electrical charges in tiny Alexandra's heart weren't properly formed, so Erin was directed to Doernbecher Children's Hospital where her baby could be monitored through the pregnancy.

At around thirty-five weeks, doctors became concerned when monitoring devices detected an accumulation of fluid around the baby's heart, and labor was induced. Alexandra Schuck was born in late September at Oregon Health Sciences University Hospital in Portland. She was six weeks premature, and her chances for a normal life were extremely small.

Dr. Seshadri Balaji, a pediatric cardiologist at OHSU, was aware of a new heart-regulating device called a "Microny" that had been developed by St. Jude Medical in St. Paul, Minnesota. The pacemaker was about a third the size of traditional models and was undergoing clinical trials by the Food and Drug Administration (FDA). Because early trials indicated that the tiny pacemaker worked effectively, Dr. Balaji appealed to the FDA to use the device on Alexandra.

Just a month after her birth, Alexandra was fitted with the world's smallest pacemaker, a device about the size of a quarter. The tiny instrument was fully capable of performing all the functions of a regular pacemaker and may not need to be replaced as Alexandra matures.

Dr. Balaji advised Alexandra's parents, Charles and Erin, that because of her heart problems, their daughter would always need a pacemaker, but that should have no adverse affect on her life.

At her six weeks' checkup on November 8, OHSU publicly announced the success of the world's smallest pacemaker in Alexandra, crediting the exemption allowed by the FDA.

When we met Richard Baumann, he was a retired seventy-year-old investment counselor who lived with his wife, Ellen, in a suburb of Phoenix, Arizona. Although they had lived for many years in San Francisco, Richard had clear memories of the lean years in the 1950s when he taught high school bookkeeping, mathematics, and biology in a very small town in southern Oklahoma. And he told us that he would never forget the night that a merciful angel manifested to pray along side him at the sickbed of his twenty-two-month-old daughter, Heather, who nearly succumbed to a severe case of scarlet fever.

Richard admitted that he and Ellen had married far too young. "I graduated in June of 1951 from college when I had just turned twenty," he told us. "I had a teaching contract in my pocket, had graduated near the top of my class, so I figured I knew about all there was to learn about life. I also decided that I should get right to work on a serious application of my teaching career and that it would be imprudent to waste precious time stretching a courtship into years. So I figured that it was time to get married. My sweetheart, Ellen, was just an eighteen-year-old sophomore at college, but I convinced her that she should abandon her plans to be a social worker and marry me."

While Richard may have believed that he was a learned fellow about to begin a successful teaching career, one thing neither he nor Ellen knew much about was birth control. Their first child, Heather, was born barely ten months after their wedding in July 1951.

"Teaching was not the cakewalk that I had believed it would be," Richard said. "I had to work hard to stay ahead of the smarter students, some of whom were only a couple of years younger than I was. I turned twenty-one in December, but my advanced years hardly impressed the eighteen- and nineteen-year-old seniors."

In retrospect, Richard knows that he just wasn't

there for Ellen during her pregnancy. "She had terrible morning sickness every morning as I was rushing to get dressed and get off to the high school," he said. "In my lack of maturity, I came to resent her heaving in the bathroom while I was trying to shave and get ready. Plus, she didn't have my breakfast ready for me the way my mother had always had Dad's waiting for him when he came in from morning chores on the farm."

Richard's teaching salary in those days was barely enough to meet the rent on their apartment and buy groceries. During summer vacation from school, he had to get another job and the one he managed to obtain with a highway road crew kept him away from home until weekends.

"Ellen began to feel that she had made the wrong choice dropping out of college," Richard said, "and I was too thick-headed to consider her valid complaint as anything other than whining. Matters only got worse when she became pregnant again."

When he resumed high school teaching that September, Richard and Ellen were barely speaking. "We had both been brought up in that old-time religion that regarded divorce as a one-way ticket to damnation, so we lived out the days and nights in a kind of cold war zone."

To make matters worse at home, Richard had barely

spent any quality time with little Heather before their son Dean was born.

"At first I thought she was just a fussy baby," he said. "Then I realized she was frightened of me because she really didn't know who the heck I was."

Richard began spending more time with his little daughter, and he was astonished to behold how just a small investment of time brought the dividends of bonding. Heather was nearly two, and he was just beginning to comprehend the rewards of being a father, of loving a child and feeling that love being returned many times over.

And then, just as Heather and baby Dean were becoming his world and he was truly developing an appreciation for both fatherhood and the remarkable qualities of his wife, his daughter came down with a severe case of scarlet fever.

Small-town doctors still made house calls in those days, and Richard and Ellen stood helplessly at Heather's bedside as Doc Murcheson stuck needle after needle of penicillin into their little daughter. Regretfully, however, the medication did not appear to be working. After several days of treatment, the doctor informed them that the illness had so ravaged Heather's little body that they should begin to prepare for the worst.

"The nearest hospital where some doctor might be

able to do Heather some good was over a hundred miles away," Richard recalled. "And Doc Murcheson as much as said that it was unlikely that Heather could stand the trip."

One night after he had insisted that Ellen get some rest, Richard sat in the midnight stillness at Heather's bedside, wondering if she would get well. For a fleeting moment, he considered that she might die, but he rejected that out of hand. He could not imagine a world without his beloved daughter. He just knew that God wouldn't let her die.

But as Richard began to think about God, he became depressed. With the care of the entire universe on His shoulders, how could He possibly find time to worry about little Heather and how sick she was?

Then he really got upset worrying about whether or not he had been too sinful for God to want to heal his daughter.

Richard got down on his knees and began to pray at Heather's bedside. He asked God to forgive him his many sins of omission and commission, and he beseeched the Almighty Creator to heal his beloved daughter in spite of what a jerk Richard Baumann might have been.

It was at that point that Richard became slowly aware of a soft blue light at the foot of Heather's bed.

"As I watched in astonishment, I saw the form of a beautiful angel beginning to take shape before my eyes," Richard said. "As the image became clearer, I saw that he—or she—was also kneeling in prayer."

Richard was mesmerized as the angelic entity appeared to grow in physical form.

"The marvelous being soon appeared as solid as the bed," Richard said. "In the soft blue light I could see that the angel's features were very solemn, almost sad. I felt as though he must be the bearer of sad news. I became increasingly frightened that he had come to take Heather with him to heaven."

Panic-stricken, Richard did not know what to do.

Should he call for Ellen? He didn't want Heather to die without her mother having been able to say good-bye to her and tell her how much she loved her.

Should he speak to the angel? Perhaps he could ask him for more time.

And then Richard noticed that when the angel's head was not bowed in prayer, the luminous being would turn his gaze upward to the ceiling, as if importuning God to listen to his prayer.

"That's when I realized that the angel was praying along with me for Heather to get well!" Richard said.

Richard knows that there was much more to the angel's prayer, but he has always remembered this portion: "Most Merciful Lord of Hosts, allow this child to continue her life on Earth. Keep her ever steadfast in the Light and keep her always from the darkness. Most Divine Lord of Heaven and Earth, remove the sickness from her body and allow her to attain her full lifespan."

All the while the angel was praying, Richard felt tears of joy coursing down his cheeks. He knew that Heather was going to be healed by the love of her guardian angel.

Then the angel was once again becoming one with the soft blue light that Richard had first noticed at the foot of his daughter's bed.

"Just before the beautiful heavenly being disappeared, I saw him smile," he said, "and I knew for certain that Heather was going to be all right."

Richard fell into a deep sleep the moment he slumped back into the chair at Heather's bedside. When Ellen awakened him the next morning, he saw that little Heather lay drenched in sweat.

"We both gave thanks to God that her fever was broken," he said. "Ellen took Heather's temperature and said that it was normal."

Richard told Ellen of the visitation of a heavenly being they assumed was Heather's guardian angel. In the next few days, Heather's condition improved steadily, and it was apparent that the prayers of her angel intercessor had been answered. Today, Heather lives with her husband in the Santa Barbara area and is the mother of three children.

Richard concluded his inspirational story by telling us that the powerful image of the angel that had prayed for Heather to get well prompted him to begin a practice that he continues to the present day. He began the spiritual discipline of tithing, returning 10 percent of whatever one had acquired that week to the Lord. That first Sunday in church, Richard's tithe was less than a dollar. Over the years, as the Lord saw fit to allow him to prosper, Richard assured us that his weekly tithe had been considerably higher.

While few adults have memories stretching back before they were four or five years of age, we have received accounts from a number of men and women who claim that they are able to recall dramatic near-death experiences (NDEs) that they experienced as young as two or three. Because both of us had near-death experiences as children, we have taken a personal interest in such reports and questions related to childhood NDEs have always been a part of the questionnaire that we devised in 1968 to probe mystical experiences in the lives of ordinary people. Of the approximately 30,000 respondents to the questionnaire thus far, 69 percent stated that they underwent a near-death experience—82 percent of that number had an NDE before the age of twelve.

Even after so many years of researching the endlessly fascinating phenomenon of mystical, spiritual, and paranormal experiences, we continue to be intrigued by the extreme youth of some of the children reporting NDEs.

A respondent to our questionnaire claimed to remember being held in his mother's arms when he was running a very high fever during a bout of chicken pox when he was two years old. "I can still clearly remember a bright light shining over my mother's shoulder," he told us in his account of the experience. "And then the light was transformed into the image of a beautiful lady. She took my hand and we went to somewhere very peaceful with lots of animals. It was like a kind of wonderful garden or the ultimate petting zoo. Then, after I don't have any idea how long, I opened my eyes to see my mom and dad smiling at me. Obviously, that was when my fever broke and I started to get better."

Another respondent insisted that she recalled an experience of falling into a lake and drowning when she was about twenty months old. "I remember that I was suddenly surrounded by lots of little boys and girls who were smiling and laughing and holding out their hands to me," she said. "Behind them was a tall, bearded man, who just seemed to beam love and peace. He smiled at me and shook his head, indicating that I couldn't stay there with the other happy children. The next thing I knew, some strange man was kneeling over me and I was coughing up water. My mom stood behind him, looking scared and relieved at the same time."

"I had already been given the last rites by our priest," wrote a questionnaire respondent. "I was twenty-six months old. Somehow I knew that I was dying. My parents were at my bedside, and my mother was weeping in deep, sobbing gasps. An angel—or a being of Light that I assumed was an angel—appeared beside me, smiled, and took me out of my body. This being told me that I would not die, that I would return to my parents and grow into a mature woman. Later, the being said that I would bear children of my own. And then I heard a nurse telling someone to get the doctor, that I was coming back to life."

Dr. Melvin Morse, author of the books *Closer to the Light* and *Transformed by the Light,* has remarked that the near-death experiences of children are special because children talk from the heart and are relatively free of cultural contamination. When children relate an account of an NDE, they do so simply, purely, unfiltered. And they are more unlikely to have an undeclared agenda of proving a particular religious belief or a preconceived spiritual expectation.

Many children describe going into the Light and then being told by a heavenly entity to go back because it is not yet their time to stay on the other side. Other children have said that they were given a choice and were able to make their own decision whether or not to stay in another level of reality. Dr. Morse has observed that it is the wise child who returns understanding that life has a purpose. As one near-death patient told him, "Life is for living. The Light is for later."

In his book *In Search of the Dead*, Jeffrey Iverson, the host of a British television series on the paranormal, tells of a five-year-old boy named Mark who startled his parents by recounting a near-death experience that he had survived at the age of *nine months.* His heart had stopped in the hospital while he was an infant. His parents certainly knew that, but they were completely unaware of their son's extraordinary experience at that time.

Mark told them that he remembered crawling down a tunnel toward a bright light. He saw doctors and nurses, his grandfather, and his mother below him, but a kind of wall separated them from him.

After he crawled through the tunnel for quite some time, a helping hand lifted him up to a place where the light was extremely bright. At this point, Mark was no longer crawling, but seemed to be gliding or floating. He remembered seeing crowds of white figures, golden roads, and even God. The boy said that God had spoken to him telepathically and asked him if he wanted to return to Earth.

Although he told God that he wanted to stay in the Light, God informed Mark that he had a purpose in life and needed to return. And then he was back in the hospital where he remained in a coma for three months.

The boy's parents told Iverson that their son's startling disclosure came about quite innocently one day during lunchtime conversation when Mark asked them, "Did you know I died?"

Their immediate response was, "Oh, really?" but Mark went on to supply such an extraordinary amount of details concerning his surgery, the environment of the hospital room, and the medical personnel that they became convinced that their son had truly observed the events from an out-of-body vantage point.

A Gallup poll conducted in 1992 indicated that around 13 million American adults claimed to have undergone at least one NDE. A survey undertaken by *U.S. News & World Report* magazine revealed that a total of 18 percent (approximately 40 million adults) of the U.S. population had undergone a near-death experience. Our friend Dr. P.M.H. Atwater, author of many studies of NDE, including *Beyond the Light,* said that nearly one-third of all those who face death in a hospital or a clinical setting are likely to have an NDE.

"With children, however, the figure is 75%," she said, citing the research of Dr. Melvin Morse, who together with Kimberly Clark Sharp and a team of associates, conducted the first empirical study of children's near-death experiences. Dr. Atwater has also spent many years investigating the near-death phenomenon, and she has found that ". . . even newborns can have a near-death experience and tell their parents when old enough to be proficient at language."

As incredible as it may seem, John Lione of Brooklyn, New York, recalled an at-birth near-death experience.

"My mother said my birth was a difficult one," Lione told us. "I was what they call a 'blue baby.' They didn't bring me to her for two days. My face was all black and blue, and I had two black eyes. She said it looked like the skin had been pulled off my face. That was where the forceps had cut me up. They had to give me a tracheotomy so I could breathe. I am also completely deaf in my right ear. As if that wasn't enough, I came down with measles when I was about six months old."

From his earliest childhood, John could remember a recurring dream that always began and ended in the same way.

"I would be kneeling down, all bent over. I am frantically trying to untie knots in some kind of rope. I am just starting to get free of the rope when I get punched in the face."

At first little John would wake up crying. Later, as he became conditioned to the nightmare, he would be able to sleep through it.

"The dream would then go on to the part where I can see this bright light coming at me from my right. Then, when I look to my left, I see this woman in a long, flowing gown. I cannot see her features clearly, but I know that she is not my mother. At the same time, I know that I know her. I also feel a great urgency to reach her. I call and call to her, but I can't seem to get to her. And that's where the dream would end."

For years John told the repetitive dream to friends and to health care professionals. No one seemed to have a clue as to what particular meaning the dream held for him.

In 1986 he had his gall bladder removed, and John

experienced the bizarre dream for the last time.

John had decided that the nightmare of ropes and knots and floating women in gowns and bright lights would always remain one of his personal mysteries when he chanced across a copy of Dr. Melvin Morse's book *Closer to the Light* in a most peculiar way.

"I was walking to work on a rainy day when I saw this book lying on the ground, dry, like someone had just dropped it," John said. "I didn't see anyone around who might be its owner, so I picked it up.

"That night when I started reading it, I was amazed to find stories of children who had had weird dreams somewhat similar to mine. My wife said that maybe I hadn't been dreaming after all. Maybe I had been having a memory of a near-death experience. The rope with the knots was when I struggled in the womb with the umbilical cord. Getting punched in the face is when the doctor grabbed me with the forceps. Then I believe that I died — and after that I went into the light."

Sometime later, John attended a conference at which Betty Eadie, author of *Embraced by the Light,* was speaking and relating her own near-death experiences.

"Afterward, when I was speaking to Betty, she mentioned seeing heavenly beings spinning material out of some bright substance," John said. "Dr. P.M.H. Atwater was there, and she said that she believed the substance to be 'spun light.' That's when I knew what the woman in the long, flowing gown had been wearing. It was a gown made of 'spun light.'"

Dr. P.M.H. Atwater also said that very young children often speak of an "animal heaven" through which they must pass before they can be in the heaven where people are. "Often children in the death experience encounter a sibling who died before them—even if that sibling was an aborted fetus. Sometimes, future siblings yet unborn are met during the child's NDE."

Dr. Atwater told us of a case that she had investigated in which a four-year-old boy reported a near-death experience after having drowned and been resuscitated. His mother may have been somewhat skeptical until he told her that he had met his brother while he was on the other side. "Brother, honey?" she questioned him. "You know that you don't have a brother."

Her little boy totally shocked her when he replied, "Yes, I do, Mommy. He was pulled from your tummy when you were only fourteen."

The woman was stunned, Dr. Atwater said. "It was true. She had become pregnant and had an abortion when she was fourteen. She had never told anyone—not her husband, not even her parents."

*T*wenty-nine-year-old Susan Sanchez, who lives in a small town near Austin, Texas, has always been an extremely religious person. Each night at bedtime she joins hands with her children, Annette and Joseph, and says their goodnight prayers to Jesus and Mother Mary aloud together.

"And every night before I go to my own bed with my husband, I always pray that the angels will protect our home from all evil and all harm, especially from fire," Susan said.

When she was just a girl of nine, Susan's aunt, Lupe

Jimenez, who had reared her after Susan's parents had died in an automobile accident, lost her beautiful home to a terrible fire that also left her horribly burned and scarred. Since that time, Susan had an overwhelming fear of fire.

Susan Sanchez's story of her baby miracle occurred one November night in 1997, when she was seven months pregnant with Joseph. She had just returned from the neighborhood supermarket when she began to smell smoke.

"Annette, who was almost four, was helping me put away the groceries when I detected the acrid scent of smoke," Susan recalled. "At first I was afraid that it was our house that was on fire, and I prayed to Jesus to deliver us from harm."

She searched through their home, looking in every room for any sign of fire. When she couldn't find any source for the smoke in her own home, Susan stepped outside. She was horrified when she saw smoke and flames coming from the Andolinos' home, just a few doors away. Susan knew that a family of six lived in the house with the wife's elderly mother, Mrs. Garza.

Susan glanced around the front yard of the Andolinos' home and saw that other neighbors were helping George Andolino, three of the children, and Mrs. Garza from the house. They all looked as though they were in bad shape from smoke inhalation. Susan knew that Linda Andolino worked nights, so at first it appeared as though everyone was present and accounted for.

But then one of the Andolino children started coughing violently and waving his arms wildly. "Dommy . . . Dommy is still upstairs!"

George Andolino had collapsed on the sidewalk, but he tried to get back to his feet. "Dear Jesus, Mary, and Joseph," he cried out, "Domingo is still in the upstairs bedroom."

Susan felt a shiver of horror move through her body. Domingo was only two years old. He might have already succumbed to smoke inhalation or been burned to death by the flames that were now spewing from every window. Great black billows of smoke rose skyward. The house was a raging inferno.

Susan heard someone near her among the neighbors gathered in the Andolinos' yard say, "It's awful. The little one trapped up there. Too late to save him now."

Someone else shouted: "The fire department. They will soon be here."

"But it will be too late to save Domingo!" another voice decreed grimly.

And then Susan heard another voice speaking directly to her: "Susan, you must save that little boy. You must enter the flames. It is up to you!"

Susan's knees felt weak and her heart pounded at her chest. How could she of all people walk into that blazing furnace? She had had a fear of fire since she was a child. Plus, just in case the *voice* hadn't noticed, she was seven months pregnant, very big, and moving with a decidedly awkward gait.

And then she thought of the Hebrew children thrown into the fiery furnace and how the Lord had kept them safe and untouched by the flames.

At the same time, Susan felt some kind of force drawing her toward the bright orange flames that curled around the rear of the house and snaked up to the second floor.

She remembered praying, "Lord, thy will be done!" And then she allowed the force to continue to pull her, frightened and trembling, into the burning house.

"It could only have been the hand of Jesus that moved me up a flight of stairs that was totally obscured by thick, black, suffocating smoke," Susan said. "Somehow I sensed that the fire had started in the kitchen, perhaps when grease caught fire and ignited the cupboards above the stove."

She was nearly to the top of the stairs when Susan gagged and choked on the thick smoke that rolled around her. She gasped for air, and all of her survival reflexes demanded that she turn back.

But the voice was insistent: *"You must go on, Susan. The life of a little boy depends on you."*

Once again Susan could feel the force moving her up the stairs. She began to cough as the smoke filled her lungs and stung her eyes.

"Cover your face with your jacket!" The voice told her.

Susan did as the voice advised her, and she finally reached the room where she could see little Domingo lying on a bed.

"I thought he was already dead from smoke inhalation, because he lay so very still—but amazingly, he was only sleeping soundly," Susan said.

She shook the two-year-old boy awake and shouted, "Fire! Fire! We've got to get out of here—or we're going to die!"

Susan helped Domingo get to his feet and ushered him to the stairs. But when the boy saw the flames and the smoke swirling around them, he began to cry and to cough.

"There was nothing to do but to pick him up and carry him down the stairs," Susan said. "I draped my jacket over both of our heads, and I kept talking to Dom and praying to Jesus all the way down the stairs. It was really like an inferno in the house, and I was fearful that I might breathe in too much smoke and collapse. It was only my prayers to Jesus and feeling heavenly love surround me that enabled me to keep moving down the stairs."

Within a few minutes, Susan stumbled outside to safety with Domingo clutched tightly to her chest.

Two or three minutes later, the fire truck arrived, along with its crew of professional firefighters. Susan was more than happy to relinquish the task of extinguishing the flames to their expertise. She had done all that the voice had asked her to do, and she handed little Domingo over to the arms of his grateful father. George Andolino declared Susan to be a heroine, truly guided by the saints.

The neighbors were quick to agree that Susan had put her life—and the life of her unborn child—on the line to save little Domingo. One of the neighbors had gone to get Linda Andolino from her job as a waitress at a truck stop, and after she arrived home and checked on her family, she embraced Susan and told her that she would be forever in her debt. One of the volunteers in the fire department called Susan a true hero.

Susan only shrugged and accepted her neighbors' thanks graciously. In her mind, she knew that the Lord Jesus to whom she prayed each night to deliver her and hers from evil and to keep fire away from their home had chosen her to act on His behalf. It was her firm and unshakable belief that it had been Jesus' voice that she had heard that had directed her to rescue little Domingo Andolino from the flames that surely would have taken his life.

"And Jesus and his angels stayed with me amidst the flames to keep Domingo and me safe from harm," she said. "When my husband Mike got home from work about an hour later and heard all the stories from the neighbors, he kissed me, patted my stomach, then crossed himself. He had tears running down his cheeks when he said that he knew our baby would be someone who would be both strong and good, for the little one had already undergone a baptism of fire. Of course, that baby was our dear son, Joseph, who has been a great blessing in our lives."

*C*het Frietag told us a remarkable story of healing that occurred after he, his wife Laurie, and their two-year-old son Mark moved to a suburb of Denver from the West Coast. They had barely finished moving into their apartment when Laurie and Mark both came down with a bad cough and a fever.

"It's my second week at work on this new job," Laurie said, fighting back tears as she crawled back into bed after checking on Mark in his bedroom. "I've got to shake this terrible bug. I can't afford to be sick right now, and I can't take the time to stay home with Mark. I have to go back to work tomorrow, and you'll have to cancel your trip so you can be with him. There is no way that Maria will come to watch Mark when he's running a fever—she won't want to bring the bug back to her kids."

"You just worry about getting better," Chet told her. "If you have to take a couple of days off, so be it."

Chet, a freelance photographer who worked out of a studio in their home and was usually happy to be "Mr. Mom" while Laurie went to the office, had accepted an assignment to film some sites of Native American ruins outside of Albuquerque, New Mexico. He had to leave the next afternoon. The financial rewards of this particular assignment were considerable, so it seemed imperative that he be able to fulfill his contract.

But the tears were moving unchecked over Laurie's cheeks. "Chet, you're well established in your field and have a great reputation. I've just started my job. I can't ask for sick leave after a week at work. They'll probably just decide to let me go."

Chet set a glass of water on the nightstand and shook two aspirin out of a bottle. "Here. Take these. And don't worry. You're good at your work, and your new bosses know it. They're not going to let you go because you caught a little flu bug."

Laurie shook her head at the aspirin. "I've taken too many of those already. Oh, Chet, this is no 'little flu bug.'

I really got sick at the office today. I had a coughing jag and nearly passed out. Shirley, one of the account directors, felt my forehead and loudly announced to everyone within hearing distance that I had a raging fever. Pretty soon everyone was asking if I wanted them to call a doctor, an ambulance, a priest."

Laurie paused to blow her nose, then continued: "I've wanted a job like this in advertising all of my adult life. Now I've probably lost it on account of I have the bubonic plague or something."

Chet knew how important the job was to Laurie, but he had accepted an advance payment on the job and was scheduled to meet with tribal leaders late the next afternoon. And he had already called Maria and asked her to come sit with Mark for a couple of days while Laurie was at work. He had made plans that he couldn't afford to alter.

As Chet left the bedroom to answer Mark's cry, he had to admit that Laurie appeared to be getting sicker by the hour. She alternated between a high fever and chills, and she seemed to have acute pains in her abdominal region. And little Mark certainly did seem to have the same nasty bug.

Chet picked up Mark to comfort him, and as he did so, Laurie called from their bedroom.

"Honey, you might as well bring him in here with

me," she said, "otherwise you're going to be up and down all night checking on him. Since Mark and I both have the same symptoms, bring him into our bed. You can sleep on the couch tonight. That's better, anyway, to help you avoid catching the flu from either of us."

Chet had to agree that it made sense to quarantine the two of them. He gently placed their son next to Laurie and adjusted the vaporizer to help the baby breathe easier.

Chet read from one of Mark's favorite books for a few minutes until it seemed as though both mother and son were sleeping. Quietly, he left the room and sat down on the couch in the living room so he wouldn't disturb them.

"I knew that we were faced with a real dilemma," Chet told us. "I knew that I couldn't leave for Albuquerque the next day and abandon Laurie and Mark. I realized that Laurie was really too ill to take proper care of our two-year-old son, and I knew that Laurie was right about Maria not wanting to come care for them for fear she would bring the flu back to her own family.

"I was really stressed," he continued, "because our finances were running on empty. Although Laurie's new firm had given her a stipend to cover moving expenses, it hadn't been nearly enough. Laurie hadn't yet received a paycheck; and as it was, without her salary and commissions my freelance work didn't give us enough money to live comfortably. Especially after Mark was born. But this job in Albuquerque would deliver a big payload, so somehow I had to leave that next morning."

Chet flipped on the television to watch one of the late-night talk shows to divert his thoughts for a few minutes from the problems swirling about his brain.

"The next thing I knew, I was jerking myself awake before I slipped off the couch and fell to the floor," Chet said. "Somehow in spite of all the stress and anxiety, I had dozed off, and my wristwatch was telling me that it was nearly two o'clock. I was only planning to watch television for a little while to clear my thoughts. I hadn't intended to fall asleep."

Chet struggled wearily to his feet and was about to check on Laurie and Mark when he had the eerie sensation that someone had entered their apartment.

"As I stood in the doorway of our bedroom, I was startled to see a tall, heavyset man leaning over Laurie," Chet said. "My heart started pounding, and I looked around for some kind of weapon to defend us both against this very large intruder. I was about to shout at him and demand to know who the blazes he was and what he thought he was doing in our apartment when I suddenly froze. There was something very peculiar about the man and the entire scenario unfolding before me.

"Then I saw that the big man was placing a hand gently, lovingly on Laurie's forehead and on Mark's chest. Now I was really confused."

As if the intruder had suddenly become aware of Chet's presence, he turned slowly and smiled at him.

"Although he had appeared as solid as a rock when I had first seen him," Chet said, "I was now able to see *through* him. He was becoming transparent right before my eyes. In spite of that, I could see clearly that he wore a bow tie and had on a three-piece suit. He was probably six feet four and about two hundred and fifty pounds.

"Just before he disappeared, he nodded at me, as if to say everything was going to be all right. A weird, luminous glow outlined his body, and he looked for a moment like the negative of a black-and-white photograph. Then he was gone."

Chet hastened to the bed where his wife and son lay sleeping. To his astonishment, they both appeared to be sleeping peacefully. The sounds of their rasping breathing had quieted.

He felt first the forehead and neck of Laurie, then of Mark—and amazingly, all traces of fever seemed to have left them.

A few minutes later, Chet slumped back onto the couch. "I didn't know what was going on," he said.

"My mind was completely blown. What or *who* had I seen? A ghost . . . an angel . . . a hallucination?

"I remember lying down on the couch to try to sort it all out. And then the next thing I knew it was morning, and I could hear that Laurie was up early, cheerfully singing her version of Neil Diamonds' greatest hits while she showered."

Bleary-eyed from lack of sleep, the peculiar events of the night before still very jumbled in his groggy brain, Chet fixed some coffee, orange juice, and toast, then picked up Mark from their bed and brought him to the breakfast table.

"Mark was giggling, seemingly free of the congestion and fever, and actually wanting to eat his bowl of oatmeal," Chet said.

Laurie cheerily entered the kitchen dressed in a sharp new business suit, ready to go to work. "Gee, honey," she said solicitously, gratefully accepting the cup of coffee from Chet's shaking fingers, "you look terrible. You should cancel your out-of-town trip. I hope you didn't catch the flu bug from us."

Chet mumbled that he would be all right and that he was pleased that she and their son had experienced such miraculous recoveries. He was about to tell Laurie about his mysterious encounter of the previous evening when she began excitedly to share a special dream.

"I had a wonderful dream that my grandfather came to see me last night," Laurie said as she sipped the hot coffee. "When I was a little girl, Poppa was always so attentive to me when I was sick. He was a high school football coach, but I told him that he should have been a doctor. I so wish that you could have met him."

Chet was aware that both of Laurie's grandparents had died when she was very young. To his knowledge, he had never even seen photographs of the couple.

"You know, honey, Poppa really had a true healing touch," Laurie told him. "Whenever he would put one of his big hands on my forehead, I would feel better right away. Poppa was so big, he was like a giant to me. I think he was so big that he just frightened away all the bad things that troubled me. Didn't matter what was bothering me — stomachache, headache, a skinned knee, measles, mumps — didn't matter at all. Poppa's touch could always make me feel better."

Intrigued, Chet asked his wife to describe her grandfather. When she finished, he told her quietly that he had seen the image of a very large man who fit that description in their bedroom at around two o'clock. He had seen the man put his hand on her forehead and on Mark's chest. And then the mysterious intruder had disappeared. Like a ghost.

Laurie began to weep. She walked to a dresser,

pulled out a small photo album, and showed Chet a photograph of a tall, heavyset man in a three-piece suit holding a little girl. "Poppa and me," she said, her voice breaking. "I was five or six."

Chet nodded. It was unquestionably a picture of the ghostly gentleman that he had seen in their bedroom.

"Poppa died in a car and train collision when I was only eight," she said. "But just two days before he was killed, the two of us were alone in the kitchen having cookies and milk. I was sitting on Poppa's lap. He hugged me and told me that he would always be with me. If I ever needed his help, he would be there.

"I loved him so much, I was traumatized by his death. I barely spoke for months after he died. Grandma missed him, too. She died two months later."

Chet took his wife into his arms and held her while she wept.

"I guess your grandfather intends to keep his word never to leave you," he said gently. "Last night I saw him place his hand on your forehead and draw out the fever. Then he reached over and somehow applied the same wonderful healing energy to Mark."

In concluding his fascinating account, Chet told us that he was absolutely certain that he had not been dreaming when he saw the apparition of Laurie's grandfather at her bedside. Then, of course, there were the miraculous recoveries of Laurie and Mark after the spirit's visitation.

Chet explained further that he and Laurie had been married for four years at the time of the miracle healing. It was the second marriage for both of them, and they had known each other for only seven months before they decided to get married. Chet had met Laurie's mother, who lived back east in Massachusetts, and Laurie's sister from Ohio when he and Laurie got married in Los Angeles. Laurie had met Chet's parents, who lived in southern California, at the same time.

"We had never really taken the time to sort out relatives beyond the immediate family," Chet said, "so I had never seen a picture of her grandfather before I saw him that night in his etheric form. I hope that he will visit us again, for he is obviously a very loving spirit. Next time, though, I hope none of us are desperately ill."

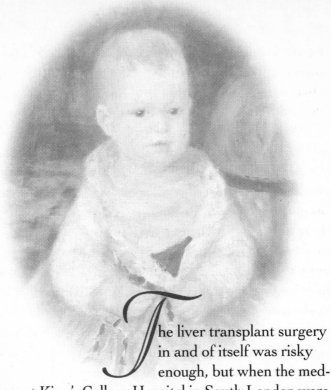

*T*he liver transplant surgery in and of itself was risky enough, but when the medical team at King's College Hospital in South London were in the midst of the operation, they discovered that twenty-six-year-old Maggie Jacock was four months pregnant.

The surgical team found themselves facing a life-or-death dilemma. If they continued with the transplant procedure, the antirejection medications Maggie would require after the surgery would be likely to kill the unborn baby. If they halted the liver transplant, then they would surely condemn Maggie to death. She had caught hepatitis two years before and it had developed into a serious liver disease. She had been weakening by the day when King's College Hospital contacted her and gave her the news that a liver had become available for transplant.

Dr. Roger Williams, head of the surgical team, quickly consulted with Maggie's husband, Paul, and the decision was made to continue with the transplant surgery. Paul was astonished to learn that Maggie was pregnant. The couple already had a two-year-old daughter, and they had wanted another child until the problems with Maggie's liver disease had arisen. Apparently the almost continual nausea brought on by her illness had masked other signs of impending motherhood, such as morning sickness; and even all the many blood tests to which she had been subjected had not detected signs of pregnancy. Although Maggie's weight gain had been considerable, it had been attributed to fluid buildup, rather than pregnancy.

When Maggie regained consciousness after the surgery, she was even more surprised to learn that she was pregnant than Paul had been. Although the doctors could make no guarantee of the baby's surviving the barrage of antirejection drugs that Maggie would soon undergo, they did inform her that the baby, a little girl, had endured the rigors of the surgery and was still alive.

Maggie desperately wanted another child, but she

accepted the doctors' caution that the drugs that they would be pumping into her would be liable to destroy the baby. Matters took an even more serious turn for the worse when Maggie caught a virus and required an even broader spectrum of drugs.

And yet, miraculously, regular medical tests indicated that the unborn girl was developing normally. Somehow she remained unscathed by the drugs that flowed through her mother's body.

In March 1994, five and a half months into her pregnancy, Maggie was able to go home with Paul and their two-year-old daughter, Hayley.

In April, Maggie gave birth prematurely to Rebecca, who weighed only two pounds, thirteen ounces. Although tiny, the miracle baby had already demonstrated that she was determined to enter the life of the Jaycock family regardless of the obstacles placed in her path.

Within a brief period of time, mother and child were sent home where they both continued to do well.

Dr. Roger Williams told reporter John Cooke that the survival of Maggie and Rebecca qualified as a miracle and as a first in the annals of surgery. According to Dr. Williams, this was the first time that a pregnant woman underwent a liver transplant and was able to deliver a healthy baby that survived unaffected by either the surgery or the antirejection drugs.

On August 4, 1998, when she was only one day old, Jazmyn Hope Stumpf, who was born with her heart outside her body, underwent a five-hour operation to have the organ placed in her chest cavity. The team of surgeons at Children's Hospital of Wisconsin in Wauwatosa, led by Dr. Bert Litwin, had to move other organs around in Little Jazmyn's chest in order for her heart to fit into the place where it belonged.

In Jazmyn's case, her heart was free-floating, connected to her body by four major blood vessels: the aorta, pulmonary artery, and superior and inferior venae cavae. Her heart was also rotated, with the apex pointing upward.

Jazmyn's parents, Marcie and Jeff Stumpf of Portage, Wisconsin, had been married for about two years when they learned that Marcie was pregnant. The Stumpfs had a fifteen-month-old daughter, and they each had children from previous marriages.

About halfway through thirty-five-year-old Marcie's pregnancy, ultrasound disclosed the baby's heart condition, known as ectopia cordis. According to American Heart Association statistics, this rare condition occurs in only 5.5 percent to 7.9 percent of 1 million live births.

On July 20, Marcie was hospitalized at Froedtert Memorial Lutheran Hospital in Wauwatosa. She was given medications to halt her labor, but when labor began again on August 3, the doctors decided to perform a cesarean section because of the high risk to the fetus.

At thirty-five weeks, five weeks short of full-term, Jazmyn weighed five pounds, one ounce. Dr. Meg Autry performed the cesarean section at Froedtert Memorial, and soon after birth, Jazmyn was brought to Children's Hospital for the delicate surgery by Dr. Bert Litwin and his team of four surgeons. Dr. Litwin had previously performed three such surgeries, two at Children's Hospital.

Although risks are high in such operations, Dr. Litwin felt that Jazmyn's heart was strong. He did advise that she would always have to be more careful than other children, however, for Jazmyn was also born without a sternum, the protective bone in front of her heart.

On August 16, 2000, Tyler Todd was born with his heart beating outside his chest and underwent intricate surgery at Rush-Presbyterian-St. Luke's Medical Center in Chicago. Although Tyler spent the first year of his life in the hospital, his surgeon Dr. Joseph Amato told the *Chicago Sun-Times* that he believed the little boy would be able to lead a normal life.

Dr. Amato also explained that after Tyler's sixth birthday, he would have to undergo more surgery to build a breastbone to protect his heart. The doctor also expected that Tyler would be required to undergo yet another such surgery later in his teen years.

C indy Donohue of Las Vegas, Nevada, told us of a most interesting experience that she and her son Allan underwent in August 1998 when he was two years old.

Allan had vomited one afternoon after lunch, and then it seemed as though in a matter of twenty minutes or so, he was running a fever of 106 degrees!

Cindy was thankful for the nurse's training that she had received before she decided to go into teaching, rather than nursing. She quickly started putting Allan in ice packs and gave him some vitamin C and baby aspirins. During the evening his fever would drop down to 104; then it would go back up to 106.

Her husband was out of town on business, so Cindy brought Allan into bed with her so she could keep a watchful eye on him all through the night. She continued to apply cold-water cloths to him periodically throughout the long hours of darkness, and the next morning the two-year-old's fever was nearly gone.

At eleven-thirty that morning, she was holding Allan in her arms, relieved that his fever appeared to have broken.

"Allan was lying across my lap, staring up at the ceiling, when all of a sudden he began to laugh," Cindy told us. "He started to say over and over, 'Pretty . . . pretty . . . light.' Then he made a horrible face, breathed in forcefully, and screamed at the top of his lungs."

Cindy became anxious. What was her son seeing that she could not?

In the next moment, Allan startled his mother with another awful scream. "No . . . no!" he cried. "Allan not go away. Stay with Mommy! Want stay with Mommy!"

Cindy hugged Allan close to her and told him that he didn't have to go anywhere. He was staying right there with her.

She felt his forehead and was alarmed that his fever seemed once again to be climbing upward.

Allan jolted her with another scream; then he smiled, just as he had done before, and said, "Light loves Allan."

He seemed quiet and contented, but then all of a sudden, Allan clutched her arm and cried out, "No, no, Mommy! Don't want to go away! Please keep Light away from me! Please keep away!"

Cindy felt a shiver of fear go through her. "I suddenly recalled what I had heard from some friends at work who did quite a bit of reading in areas of spirituality and metaphysics," she said. "From time to time during coffee breaks they had spoken of people saying that they were 'going into the Light' when they were dying. Dear God, I thought, was Allan dying? Was he seeing a being of Light coming to take him to the other side?"

Cindy got up and carried Allan into the bathroom. "I ran a tub of cold water and submerged his little body, holding firm against his struggles and his cries for me to stop. I knew that I had to break that fever."

After a few minutes, Cindy toweled her shivering son dry and checked his temperature. It was once again beginning to lower.

"Although I had never been what one could call a religious person," Cindy admitted, "I began to pray to God that Allan's fever would drop and that whatever malignant flu bug had got hold of him would soon release its grip. At the same time, I asked that if He had sent angels to come to take Allan to Heaven, that they go away and leave us alone."

Cindy checked Allan again after about fifteen minutes and was relieved to find that his temperature had dropped to 100 degrees.

"Allan hugged me very tight, then came out of it altogether," Cindy said. "Somehow I knew that the worst of it was over. I knew then that his sickness had passed, that his dangerously high fever was leaving him."

Cindy told us that from time to time she would talk to Allan about the Light. He remembered the experience clearly for quite some time, but each time she asked him about it, the encounter with the Light seemed to fade a bit in his memory.

"Now Allan is six, and when I talk about it, he seldom appears to know to what I am referring," Cindy said. "But when I look back on the experience, I am certain that we nearly lost Allan. I think he came close to dying. I am just very thankful that the Light wasn't yet ready to claim my little son."

*L*ogan Carroll was born on 4:42 P.M., April 6, 1995. Tragically, he was not breathing and his heart had stopped.

Tami Carroll, Logan's mother, a twenty-eight-year-old accountant from Nabb, Indiana, had been worried from the moment that she had gone into labor. She had lost a child at birth in 1993, but she kept reassuring herself that everything about her pregnancy with Logan had been normal. And just before the birth, Logan's heart rate had been monitored as normal.

Nothing should have gone wrong—but it had.

While Tami tried her best to remain calm and be positive, obstetrician Diana Okon began using all of her considerable skills as a physician to bring little Logan back to life.

But at 5:15 P.M., Dr. Okon and the obstetrics team at Clark Memorial Hospital in Jeffersonville, Indiana, ceased their efforts to revive Logan. He still showed no sign of a heartbeat, and his skin had turned a bluish gray color.

Caring nurses wiped the baby clean, wrapped him in a blanket, put a little cloth on his head, and handed Logan to Tami so that she might say good-bye.

Tami remembered that tears had streamed down her face, and she felt overwhelming sadness. She had already lost one baby at birth. And now she had carried Logan nine months and had lost him at the very last moment.

The sympathetic nurses in the delivery room abandoned their professional demeanor and began to weep along with the heartbroken mother. Tami's husband, Todd, and her sister and mother entered the delivery room to say their final good-byes to little Logan.

Tami's mother was the last to cradle Logan in her arms, and it was as she was holding him that she felt and saw that he had begun to breathe.

In response to the grandmother's excited cries of joy, a nurse placed her finger on Logan's chest and verified that she felt a heartbeat.

Dr. Okon was summoned, astonished that a full hour and eighteen minutes had passed since the child had been born dead. When she entered the delivery room and saw that Logan's color had changed from lifeless blue-gray to a pink, glowing, full-of-life hue, she pronounced that he was, indeed, quite alive.

The word spread throughout the hospital, and within minutes the delivery room was crowded with wide-eyed doctors, each verifying that the baby born dead had a heartbeat and was breathing effortlessly.

Just to be certain, Logan was transferred to Kosair Children's Hospital in nearby Louisville, Kentucky, for close monitoring. The baby was given some medication and oxygen, but he really required no special treatment. On May 10, Tami and Todd Carroll took their miracle baby home with them.

Tami told reporters James McCandlish and Don Gentile that she and her husband recognized the reality that God had granted them a miracle in restoring their son to life and they gave daily thanks for the blessing.

Dr. Diana Okon said that there really was no medical explanation for a baby's coming back to life after dying during childbirth and remaining dead for a full hour and eighteen minutes. Dr. Okon agreed that Logan's resurrection was "an honest-to-God miracle."

When witnesses arrived at the scene of a crash a few miles outside of Lincoln, Nebraska, on a hot July afternoon in 1997, they assumed that both the woman behind the wheel and the infant in the baby seat had been killed outright by the drunk driver who had rammed a pickup into their car and pushed it onto the shoulder of the highway. While someone called 911, others tried to free the mother and child from the wreckage.

And then the car burst into flames. The woman, barely conscious, had cried out for someone to free her baby from the backseat.

By the time rescue workers and highway patrol offi-
cers arrived on the scene, Marcia Kraus was enveloped
in flames. Although her baby was terribly burned, eight-
month-old Jeff was still alive when a paramedic managed to pull him from the car.

The woman responsible for the accident was walking
around her truck, dazed but seemingly unhurt. As far as
the highway patrolman questioning her could determine,
she appeared more concerned over her husband's likely
anger over wrecking his new pickup than the grim fact
that she had killed a person . . . perhaps two.

Before they loaded the baby into an ambulance, one
of the paramedics told an investigating officer that he
doubted if the little boy would survive. Their initial
examination suggested the infant had quite possibly been
fatally burned.

When Tom Kraus arrived home from work that
afternoon at the real estate agency and heard the message on the answering machine from a nurse at the Burn
Center of the Memorial Hospital to call back as soon as
possible, he could only guess what horrible thing had
happened to his wife and son. Tom knew that Marcia
was going to visit her mother in a nearby suburb that
afternoon and that she had planned to be home in time to
fix dinner. He had already become a bit concerned when

he pulled into the driveway and noticed that Marcia's car was not parked in the garage.

Just as Tom was about to dial the number left by the nurse, a highway patrol officer was at the front door, somberly informing him of Marcia's death and of the injuries sustained by their son, Jeff. While the officer remained for a few minutes to allow Tom to compose himself, Tom called the nurse and learned that little Jeff's injuries were extremely serious.

After the officer had gone, Tom made a tearful call to his mother-in-law and informed her of the accident. Then he called his brother Ron and asked him to drive him to the hospital.

Dr. R. Marshall Hirsch, director of the Burn Center, warned Tom to prepare himself for the worst. It appeared unlikely that little Jeff would be able to survive the serious burns that he had sustained. In layman's terms, Dr. Hirsch explained that the extensive burns were literally sucking the life-giving fluids from Jeff's tiny body.

"I will do all that I can to save your son's life," Dr. Hirsch said, "but his condition is extremely serious. I need your help, Tom. You must participate in Jeff's healing to the fullest extent of your ability. You must really be there for him—mentally, emotionally, and physically. He needs to hear your voice. He needs to know that you are here with him."

Tom made a vow to his brother and to his mother-in-law, Sandra Edel, that he was not going to give up on Jeff. Later, he said, he would take the time to grieve for his beloved wife. Now he needed to be there for Jeff. Tearfully, Tom stated that he knew that he would best honor Marcia's memory by exerting all the love and willpower that he had to keep their little son alive.

For the next several months, while his eight-month-old son fought to maintain a hold on life, Tom spent hours at Jeff's side in the intensive care burn unit. He would lean down as close as possible and tell him how much he loved him. "Your daddy is right here beside you, Jeff," Tom said. "I'll always be here for you. It's just the two of us now, my little big man. You're going to get better. You're going to get stronger. We'll make it. We'll make it together, the two of us."

Through those long days and nights of awful pain from countless skin grafts, Tom would whisper words of love and encouragement. When there were times when he had to leave for a couple of hours to check on things at the real estate office, Tom placed a tape recorder at his little son's side that played his comforting words of love over and over again.

When his brother Ron asked Tom how he was holding up, Tom answered that he was convinced that the bond of love that he had now firmly established with Jeff would pull him through the ordeal. Tom's only regret was that he wasn't able to take upon himself some of the pain that he knew his little guy was enduring.

After a couple of months, Jeff's condition had stabilized and the doctors could begin using high-tech razors to harvest replacement skin from his little torso. Tom could hardly bear watching the procedures, knowing that the pain must have been awful for Jeff. And after the grafts had been secured, it seemed as though every time Jeff moved his skin would crack open and bleed.

At last the day came when Jeff was out of danger and was firmly on the road to full recovery. Although there would be some scars that would remain from the terrible burns that he had suffered, Jeff was able to resume life as a healthy boy with a loving and devoted father.

Tom Kraus said that while he would forever be indebted to the excellent medical staff that had saved his son's life, he knew in his heart that the ultimate deciding factor in Jeff's recovery was the bond of love that had forever been forged between them.

"My son will know always that I love him so much," Tom said. "Even later in life when he might face other situations that bring him pain or misery, he will still be able to hear my voice in his memory saying over and over again that I love him and will always be there for him."

*L*arry DuBoise, assistant engineer on Amtrak's Southwest Chief, could not believe his eyes when the passenger train rounded a sharp curve on the outskirts of Isleta, New Mexico, at 1:30 P.M. on May 16, 1992.

"My God!" he shouted to engineer John Vannoy. "There's a child on the tracks!"

As the Southwest Chief thundered toward the baby, the men watched helplessly as eighteen-month-old toddler Jeremy Abeita walked down the center of the tracks, his back to the train.

DuBoise yelled to Vannoy to slam on the emergency brakes, but both engineers knew that it would be impossible to stop the train in time to prevent hitting the child.

Vannoy blasted the horn, and the baby jumped and turned to see the train bearing down upon him.

"Baby! Baby! Get out of the way! Get off the tracks!" DuBoise shouted.

Confused and frightened, little Jeremy dropped to his hands and knees and began to crawl. DuBoise could see that the baby was trying to get off the tracks, but he knew that he could never make it before the train was upon him.

The forty-four-year-old engineer got out on the engine's front catwalk, then carefully moved down the metal stairs, wedging his legs in the bottom and second steps. He was now dangerously close to the shrieking front wheels of the locomotive and the cowcatcher—the metal frame on the engine's nose.

He grabbed a handrail, then lowered himself until his head was only about five inches above the steel tracks. His desperate plan was to attempt to catch hold of the boy and pull him out from under the crushing wheels of the train.

By the time the engine was about fifty feet from little Jeremy, it was still moving about forty miles per hour. DuBoise said later that he felt that it was God's will that he should do his utmost to save the boy, but he felt his blood freeze when he heard Jeremy scream. The cow-catcher had brushed Jeremy's body, and he fell under the metal frame toward the massive steel wheels.

DuBoise stretched out his arm in a desperate, blind attempt to grab the baby. He silently offered thanks to God when he felt his fingers clutch the infant's shoulder. With a great effort of will, he was able to pull Jeremy free and throw him onto the grassy ditch at the side of the tracks.

When engineer John Vannoy was at last able to stop the Southwest Chief, DuBoise saw the terrified mother sweeping her son up in her arms.

DuBoise remembered that he wanted to run to help her, but he stood next to the engine, rooted to the spot, as if paralyzed. He simply could not move after having accomplished the daring rescue.

A doctor and nurse who were passengers on the Southwest Chief gave Jeremy first aid before an ambulance arrived and he could be rushed to a hospital. The eighteen-month-old boy's lower left leg had been severed when he was struck by the engine, and he had also received abdominal and head injuries. But he survived.

Jeremy's mother, as well as the passengers, crew, and other witnesses of Larry DuBoise's remarkable, selfless heroism said that he had performed a miracle. DuBoise, however, gave all the credit to God. In his opinion, the Almighty had wanted him to intervene in what seemed like certain death for the boy, because He had something important for Jeremy to do in the future.

Later that year, Larry DuBoise was awarded the Carnegie Medal for heroism.

Eight-year-old Corey Preston was horrified when he saw his two-year-old brother Anthony standing between the rails of the railroad track. Apparently, little Anthony had somehow slipped away from the baby-sitter and had walked out onto the tracks near their home in Ocean Springs, Mississippi. And now there was a freight train roaring down the tracks, moving rapidly toward Anthony, less than a minute away from running over him.

Corey, who had been enjoying a workout on his rollerblades on that afternoon in May 1994, knew that it was up to him to get his little brother. Their grandmother Betty was at work, and their mother, Stephanie, who was in the Army, was in Washington, D.C., at the time.

As he sped toward the tracks on his skates, Corey yelled at Anthony to get off the rails.

But Anthony had suddenly become fully aware of the huge locomotive bearing down on him. Wide-eyed with fear, he froze.

Corey hobbled on his blades and got next to the tracks. He shouted at Anthony to take his hand so he could pull him off the rails.

The locomotive's whistle was shrieking an urgent alarm. The engineer had spotted the kids and was warning them to get off the tracks immediately. The freight train was hauling an extra number of boxcars, and it was far too big and long and moving too fast to be able to stop.

At the sound of the engine's piercing screech, Corey clambered awkwardly on the tracks, his rollerblades making him teeter clumsily.

Since Anthony seemed unable to move out of harm's way, Corey shoved his little brother off the tracks. Better a skinned knee or elbow than to be run over by a freight train, Corey had reasoned.

But then Corey found himself in a nightmarish situation. The wheels of his skates had gotten caught between the crossties on the tracks.

Panic-stricken, the eight-year-old pulled at one skate and then the other. He could hear his brother crying out in fear.

The engineer slammed on the brakes of the massive locomotive, and Corey's world was overwhelmed with the sound of metal shrieking against metal and the sight of the huge engine bearing down on him.

At the last possible second, Corey managed to pull his skates free of the track, but it wasn't soon enough to prevent him from being slammed to the ground, unconscious and bleeding.

For a few moments, little Anthony stood beside the crumpled figure of his big brother, who was lying motionless in a pool of blood. And then it was the two-year-old's turn to be heroic. He ran all the way home and alerted nearby relatives, who called an ambulance.

The boys' grandmother happened to be at the hospital when the ambulance arrived, and she was shocked to see her minister and family members walk in with Anthony.

Doctors treated Corey for a smashed pelvis and hip socket and numerous cuts and bruises, and he was released five days later. Although he would have to use crutches until his injuries mended, the boy's courageous actions in saving his little brother could well have cost him his life. Some miracles have a price attached to them, and the tag on this one could have been a great deal higher.

$\mathcal{G}$inger Price of Little Rock, Arkansas, wrote to tell us that in 1969, when she was eleven years old, she had witnessed a true miracle.

She said that she had told the story many times to many different people—some who believed, some who didn't. Whether or not her listeners believed her story mattered little to Ginger. She felt that her life and that of every member of her family changed that night in December 1969 when her mother asked God to tell the Angel of Death to leave her little son behind.

Ginger's story began when her parents adopted

Daniel, a month-old baby boy, whom all the family loved very much.

"Daniel's mother was a young waitress who worked in a restaurant in a small Arkansas village not far from the one where we lived at the time," Ginger said. "Her husband had been killed in a hunting accident when she was six months pregnant. The young mother had become very ill a couple of weeks before her delivery, and since neither she nor her husband had any family in the area, she simply could not afford to keep the baby. Mom was a nurse in the local clinic, and she had come to know the woman and her situation. Since my parents were unable to have any children after my sister Carole's difficult birth in 1965, it seemed ordained that they should take baby Daniel."

From the beginning, though, Ginger recalled, they had all been concerned about the baby's waxen pallor. For a time, the infant seemed to improve, but when Daniel was about ten months old, he developed pleurisy and his lungs became terribly congested. Ginger's parents, Martha and Rex Price, and their family doctor, Joe Beardsley, were worried that Daniel might have inherited his mother's tendency toward ill health.

On the night when the miracle occurred, Ginger remembered that she had just carried Daniel out to the sofa in the living room. The baby shared a small bedroom with three-year-old Carole, and their mother was concerned that Daniel's loud and raspy breathing would keep her awake.

"I was about to go to bed around nine o'clock when Mom and I heard a firm knock on the door," Ginger said. "Dad had a small trucking business and was out of town for a couple of nights, so we got a little nervous about who could be at our door at that time of night."

Ginger and her mother stood facing the door. "I felt a shiver go up my spine, and I could see that Mom looked really nervous," Ginger remembered. "Mom kind of crept toward the door, and she was just about to turn on the porch light to see who was outside knocking on our front door when we heard the latch of the locked door click."

Ginger and her mother stepped back in fearful caution. Someone was opening their front door without a key.

"I knew where Daddy kept his .410 shotgun," Ginger said, "and I was about to make a run for the closet in my parents' bedroom. I could only assume that any burglar or thief who was bold enough to come in through the front door when folks were still up and the lights were on was prepared to do the people inside the home some harm."

Wide-eyed with apprehension and suddenly unable to move or make a sound, they watched the door swing slowly open and a most incredible personage entered their home.

"As Mom and I watched in disbelief, an angelic figure in shining white robes entered the room and closed the door slowly behind it," Ginger said. "Without a word, this incredible being crossed the room to where Daniel lay sleeping on the sofa."

Her mother shook free of her awe-inspired paralysis, and Ginger heard her cry out: "Dear God, it's the Angel of Death come to take little Daniel! Please, dear Lord, don't take our baby boy! Please give him another chance. What can it matter to you, Master of the Universe, whether or not this heavenly being leaves with a sick little baby? Please, dear God, tell this Angel of Death to leave little Daniel alone!"

Ginger remembered clearly that the angel reached out as if to lift the baby from the sofa, then, as if it were listening to a voice beyond the human range of hearing, the being lowered its arms and turned to walk away.

"I don't know if it was Mom's supplication that caused the angel to reconsider taking Daniel, but the angel left him on the sofa that night," Ginger said. "Halfway to the door, though, the angel stopped and turned to face Mom and me. I will never forget that moment and that angelic countenance. It was absolutely the most beautiful, peaceful, loving face that anyone could ever imagine."

Ginger recalled that she was so frightened that her teeth were chattering.

Her mother finally broke the silence by asking Ginger if she, too, had seen the angel. Ginger said, "I told her that I had most certainly seen the angel and that I would never forget it if I lived to be 150—and that it had seemed to want to take Daniel away, then changed its mind."

Her mother wiped tears away from her eyes. "I think that God told the Angel of Death to give us another chance to keep little Daniel," she told Ginger.

At that moment, the baby began to moan and to toss restlessly on the sofa. For three days, two doctors sought to save Daniel's life by increasing his medications.

"On Sunday evening, while Carole was in the living room watching television and Mom was taking a nap, I sat beside Daniel's crib, keeping watch over him in the bedroom," Ginger said. "This time there was no knock at the door. The angel that came that night appeared in the blink of an eye and stood beside little Daniel and me. This angel seemed somehow younger and even more beautiful than the first one. I know angels aren't like us and show their age, but this being of glorious light seemed to appear as a strong and healthy youth."

Ginger remembered that she saw Daniel smile up at the angel. "Then the baby let out a long sigh, and the awful rasping sound left his chest. I thought that he had died. That the Angel of Death had come this time to claim his soul."

Her mother came out of her bedroom at that moment, just in time to see the angel rise through the ceiling.

"Oh, dear God," she cried out, kneeling beside Daniel's crib, making the same assumption that Ginger had made. "The Angel of Death came back to take our baby away from us!"

But then Daniel took a deep breath and opened his eyes. The angel had come to bring healing, not death.

When Martha Price took the baby to the clinic the next afternoon, Dr. Beardsley listened carefully to Daniel's chest and happily agreed with the relieved mother's diagnosis: Daniel's chest was now devoid of any sounds or signs of illness or congestion. Dr. Beardsley pronounced the rapid recovery to be a miracle.

Ginger concluded her account by stating that little Daniel, who had begun his sojourn on Earth as a sickly baby, seldom suffered another sick day all the rest of his years growing up in Arkansas.

"He entered the ministry in 1994. Rev. Daniel has a lovely wife and beautiful twin girls, who look like little angels. We will forever thank God for granting Mom her mother's prayer of life for her child," says Ginger.

*T*he tornadoes that struck Oklahoma in the first days of May 1999 left death and destruction in their wake. The early reports issued on May 6 declared 41 deaths, 55 people missing, and nearly 700 individuals injured. The account of the miracle that ten-month-old Aleah and her mother and father experienced was one story that lifted the hearts of those who had been so brutalized by the monstrous power of the twisters.

Deputy Robert Jolley was chasing one of the twisters across the mangled landscape of Grady County when he spotted a man wandering down a road, apparently in a state of shock. When Deputy Jolley stopped to question him, Robert Williams told the officer that the tornado had sucked his daughter, son-in-law, and ten-month-old baby granddaughter out of a closet where they had taken shelter.

The survivor of the frightening experience described how his wife had died in his arms when a trailer had crashed into the remaining walls of the closet. Williams was able only to hold her head in his hands and tell her good-bye as the tears rolled down her cheeks. She had been unable to speak a word before she died.

Deputy Jolley set out in search of the three victims who had been pulled from the home by the terrible suction of the twister. Perhaps by some miracle they had been spared.

About one hundred feet from what remained of the Williams's home, the officer saw what at first he thought was a rag doll in a pile of debris caught at the base of a tree. Gently, Deputy Jolley picked up the "doll," which upon closer examination, proved to be a baby girl whose eyes and ears were packed with mud. As he carefully wiped the mud from her face, little Aleah began to cry.

The sound of that baby crying made the deputy feel a wonderful surge of joy.

Deputy Jolley rushed little Aleah to the hospital where she was reunited with her mother, Amy, who by some miracle had suffered only bruises and scratches. Amy's husband, Ben Molton, had received more serious injuries, but incredibly, they had managed to survive the ordeal of having been sucked out of their home and carried away by a historic F5 tornado. A tornado is considered formidable if its damage ranks F2 or higher on the Fujita scale.

*T*wenty-four-year-old Barbara Blodgett of Yakima, Washington, was three months pregnant when she was injured in a car accident on June 30, 1988. Although she was in a coma for five months, Barbara gave birth to Simon, a healthy baby boy, on December 9. The day after her son was born, she began emerging from the coma.

Doctors were uncertain why Barbara was able to regain consciousness, but they speculated that hormonal changes after the birth might have been responsible. While her complete recovery from the brain stem

injuries suffered during the accident continued to hand-
icap her to some degree, Barbara Blodgett spelled a message for readers of *USA Today* on February 14, 1989,
when she pointed out the letters for the words: "Never
give up."

In January 1998, even though she had been in a coma
for seven months, twenty-one-year-old Ledy Minguzzi
gave birth to a healthy baby girl at Lugo Hospital in
Rome, Italy.

Ledy had suffered a brain hemorrhage when she was
one month pregnant, and to prepare her for the delivery
of her baby, neurosurgeons performed a complex
surgery that brought her into a state called "vigilant
coma." In this level of consciousness, Ledy remained
paralyzed but could communicate with the doctors by
blinking her eyes.

After the cesarean birth, Dr. Marco Mattucci placed
the five-pound, four-ounce baby girl on Ledy's breast.
According to the doctor, a single tear of joy ran down
Ledy's cheek. In Dr. Mattucci's opinion, this was a certain sign that Ledy understood what had happened. The
Vatican's newspaper, *Osservatore Romano,* said that the
surgery conducted by Dr. Mattucci and his staff was
"a masterpiece of life."

On April 24, 1999, a pregnant Maria Lopez entered a coma after complaining of headaches and nausea. Although at first the doctors at the University of California Medical Center assessed the symptoms as a result of the pregnancy, upon closer examination of their patient they discovered that Maria had been born with arteriovenous malformation, a condition in which blood vessels in the brain are malformed or tangled.

Medical personnel sought to treat Maria Lopez's condition by a process called embolization, during which the blood flow to the brain is lessened. In spite of their concerted efforts, however, Maria remained in a coma.

After three weeks had passed with no signs of improvement, doctors at the UC Medical Center advised the Lopez family that they should consider withdrawing life support. Sadly, the decision was made to do as the doctors recommended. A priest was summoned to give her last rites.

Then, just as the priest was concluding the service, Maria Lopez coughed.

The attending physicians, not wishing to appear without compassion, nevertheless told the family gathered around Maria's bed for the last rites, that her cough was only a kind of reflex.

However, the Lopez family saw their beloved Maria's movement as a sign from God. Sylvia Hernandez, Maria's sister, said that it was a sign that Maria was not ready to die, that she wanted the family to give her more time to come around.

A few days later, Dr. John Frazee, a vascular neurosurgeon at the UC Medical Center, was astonished when Maria awoke from her coma and responded to his commands. Dr. Frazee commented that whether or not Maria's cough had been a sign from God, it had saved her life, because it had convinced the Lopez family to keep her on life support.

Several days after Maria had communicated with Dr. Frazee, she slipped back into a coma. Once again, her family did not give up on her.

And it was a good thing that the Lopez family had a strong faith in God and in the eventuality of their daughter's recovery. Maria awakened again, this time for good, and six days later give birth to healthy twins.

While doctors at the Medical Center said that they could offer no explanation for Maria Lopez's recovery, Dr. Scott Strum commented that numerous studies in medical literature give credence to the idea that a nurturing, loving, and supportive family is a great factor in the recovery process.

On January 14, 2001, Shannon Kranzberg delivered her daughter Alexis while in a coma caused by a November 16, 2000, car crash in Dallas, Texas. Then, amazingly, a week later Mrs. Kranzberg awakened from the coma to find that she had given birth to a daughter.

"I just woke up, and the baby was there," Shannon told the *Dallas Morning News*. According to attending physicians, Alexis's birth was two months premature, evidently triggered by the staph infection that Shannon Kranzberg had contracted while in the hospital.

Michael Kranzberg had accepted the grim possibility that his daughter would never be born and that his wife would never regain consciousness. When Shannon and Alexis were released on March 15, Michael told the media that Shannon was his hero, and he offered their miracle as a testimony to everyone who might find themselves in their situation that they must always keep faith.

On July 23, 2001, twenty-four-year-old Chastity Cooper of Warsaw, Kentucky, gave birth to her daughter after having been in a coma since two weeks after conception. For a woman in a coma to complete the entire term of her pregnancy and give birth to a healthy child is a rare occurrence. Alexis Michelle Cooper was a healthy seven pounds, seven ounces.

Chastity, who had previously given birth to two boys, received a severe head injury in an automobile accident on the rainy night of November 25, 2000. She had dropped off the boys at her sister's and was driving to meet her husband at a family gathering when her car slid into the path of another. Routine medical tests performed during Chastity's emergency treatment at University Hospital in Cincinnati, Ohio, indicated that she was pregnant. Since it was only two weeks after conception, even her husband, Steve, hadn't known that they were about to become parents again.

Dr. Michael Hnat, an obstetrician who specializes in high-risk pregnancies, said that the pregnancy did not appear to complicate Chastity Cooper's condition. Doctors had induced labor about a week prematurely to better manage the birth and the comatose patient's welfare.

Steve Cooper told the *Cincinnati Enquirer* that little Alexis, their newborn daughter, was precious. He said that Chastity and he had wanted a daughter for a long time. Cooper also said that although his wife was not able to move or to talk, he was certain that she was aware of Alexis's birth. He had placed the baby on Chastity's side and she had smiled and established eye contact with her daughter. Cooper was convinced that a bond had been established between mother and baby.

*O*ur friend Shirley Hessel wrote to us with an account of what she believed to be the manifestation of celestial music that indicated the presence of an angel watching over her granddaughter.

Her son told her that he and his wife would frequently awaken in the middle of the night to hear music coming from somewhere in their house. The music was unlike anything they had heard. "Angel music" was the closest description that he could manage in attempting to describe the sounds to Grandmother Shirley.

On one particular night when the music awakened
the couple, they were determined to track down the
source of the "angel music."

The young couple went from room to room until they
realized at last that the music was clearly issuing from
the bedroom of their two-year-old baby daughter,
Ashley.

Once they were in her bedroom, they thought that
the sounds might be coming from a music box. They
picked up all the music boxes that little Ashley had in
her room, but not one of them was playing.

And though they knew very well that the glorious
refrains that they had been hearing were far different
from any of the familiar nursery tunes and melodies con-
tained in Ashley's music boxes, they had felt compelled
to be certain.

After their careful investigation, they were sure that
the sounds of the celestial music box were a wonderful
sign that an angel was watching over their precious
little one.

One would have to agree with Army Captain Ida Agamy when she calls their daughter Amiera their "miracle girl." When Amiera was born on August 17, 1994, doctors told her parents, Ida and Adel Agamy, that she would die within minutes if she were taken off a life-support machine. But when reporter Bill O'Neill interviewed the Agamys at their home in Falls Church, Virginia, in June of 1996, the twenty-month-old girl was of normal size and intelligence, and her heart and lungs were functioning at full performance.

Amiera, whose name in Arabic means "princess," had been born after a very difficult delivery. She was placed at once in intensive care, and when she was five days old, her heart began to fail.

Ida Agamy recalled that it seemed as though their precious little baby was put through hundreds of tests by the medical staff. And then, at the age of three weeks, it was determined that Amiera had somehow contracted an unidentified, but deadly, strain of virus. She was placed on a heart-lung bypass machine, which sustained her weakened heart and lungs.

Three weeks later, another threat to her tiny life occurred when doctors discovered that Amiera displayed signs of internal bleeding that had been caused by the blood thinners that were necessary to keep her on the bypass machine.

It was at this point of extreme despair that the doctors informed Ida and Adel Agamy that they were now forced to choose between two courses of action—neither of which was the least bit promising. They could leave Amiera on the machine, which, because of the internal bleeding, would slowly cause her to bleed to death. Or they could choose to remove her from the machine, which would cause her to die within minutes.

Since neither choice promised the eventuality of a cure, the Agamys told the doctors to take their little

Princess off the machine so that her suffering might end. Then they said their sad good-byes and sat quietly beside their daughter, awaiting what they were told was the inevitable: Amiera would surely die within minutes after being removed from the bypass machine.

But Amiera refused to recognize the medical decree. She refused to accept the doctors' ultimatum.

When the attending physician saw that Amiera had lived far longer than the few minutes that medical science had allowed her, drugs were prescribed to strengthen the little girl's heart. Now the medical consensus was that if Amiera made it for twenty-four hours, she was likely to live long enough for the doctors to arrange for a heart-lung transplant.

The Agamys sat beside her until the morning hours, recalling that night as the longest of their lives. As they sat holding her tiny little hands, they prayed that their beautiful Princess would survive the crucial next twenty-four hours.

Thanks to the earnest, loving prayers of her parents and the skillful ministrations of the medical staff, Amiera kept right on living—and her heart continued to grow stronger.

The transplant was never needed, and over the next few weeks, Amiera was gradually weaned from the medications. When she was two months and two days old, the little Princess went home with her joyful parents.

Dr. Lars Erikson, Amiera's physician at Massachusetts General Hospital, acknowledged that if someone survives against great odds, "that's a pretty good definition of a miracle."

Amiera continued to amaze the doctors with her progress. They had prepared her parents with the prognosis that because of her ordeal with the virus and the time spent on the bypass machine, their daughter would possibly be severely retarded and suffer from a host of health problems.

But when reporter O'Neill interviewed the Agamys in the summer of 1996, Amiera was learning to walk and to say a few words — and Dr. Erikson pronounced her recovery to be "excellent."

Who is the world's tiniest baby miracle? When identical twin Tyler Davison was born on June 8, 1992, at Nottingham City Hospital in England, he entered the world three months premature, weighing a featherweight eleven ounces and stretching out to just six inches. His twin, Stephen, was a hefty big brother at two pounds, two ounces.

The twins had to be brought into the world prematurely when doctors discovered during tests that they were not growing properly in the womb of their mother, thirty-one-year-old Catrina Davison. Medical experts informed Catrina and her husband, Stephen, that Tyler was receiving less of the blood flow and was extremely small. The only way to save the twins was to deliver them prematurely by a cesarean procedure.

After a week in a special incubator where oxygen equipment assisted his breathing, little Tyler was removed and was able to partake of his first meal of his mother's milk.

A spokesperson for *The Guinness Book of World Records* said that Tyler would be included in a future edition of the book, replacing Marian Chapman as the world's smallest surviving baby. Chapman, also British, was born in 1938, weighing ten ounces, one ounce less than Tyler. She was, however, twelve inches in length, twice Tyler's size.

Around the same time that Tyler was born, there was a claim that a baby had been born in Japan that weighed only 10.5 ounces, half an ounce less than Tyler.

On February 9, 1997, a close contender for the crown of World's Smallest Baby was born in Iowa City, Iowa. Alicia Allen weighed only twelve ounces and was said by her parents, Lu Ann and Harry, to be smaller than a Barbie doll. When she was released by the

University Hospital in June, Alicia weighed five pounds, five ounces—seven times her birth weight.

While the average gestation period is between thirty-eight and forty weeks, Drew McSweeney was born on April 15, 2001, after twenty-three weeks, five days. One of the smallest babies to survive in New Jersey, Drew weighed 15.6 ounces at birth at Saint Barnabas Medical Center in Livingston. Drew remained in the hospital's Perinatal Center for four months. He was released to his parents on August 5, just three days before his due date.

In February of 2002, the present uncontested winner of the World's Smallest Baby title went to a baby girl nick-named "Perla" by her medical team at the Careggi Hospital in Florence, Italy. Perla weighed only 9.97 ounces and was ten inches in length.

Born two months premature, the miniscule baby girl spent three months in intensive care. According to her doctors, Perla suffered from breathing difficulties, anemia, hypothyroidism, hypoglycemia, and jaundice. When she was released to go home in May 2002, Perla weighed 4.4 pounds and had an almost 100 percent chance of leading a normal life.

On April 1, 1991, rescue worker Hubert Haddukiewicz was astonished when he found an unharmed month-old baby girl amid the rubble of a five-story apartment house that had been blown to bits by a gas explosion.

Later, Haddukiewicz declared that little Laure Claes had to have been protected by the wings of angels to have survived a fall of fifty feet with the walls of the building crumbling all around her.

Imagine the horror of twenty-three-year-old mother Cathy Claes of Salbris, France: She had just given her